VIRGINIA SEASE
Her study of German literature led to a PhD from
the University of Southern California in 1969. She
has been a member of the Executive Council of the
General Anthroposophical Society since 1984, and
served from 1991 to 2001 as leader of the Section
for the Arts of Eurythmy, Speech, Drama and
Music of the School of Spiritual Science at the Goetheanum in Dornach
(Switzerland). Her current responsibilities include liaising between the
Executive Council and English-speaking anthroposophists around the
world, and directing the English Anthroposophical Studies Programme at
the Goetheanum.

By the same author (all with Manfred Schmidt-Brabant):

The Archetypal Feminine in the Mystery Stream of Humanity
The New Mysteries and the Wisdom of Christ
Paths of the Christian Mysteries, From Compostela to the New World
Thinkers, Saints, Heretics, Spiritual Paths of the Middle Ages

RUDOLF STEINER'S ENDOWMENT

Centenary Reflections on his Attempt for a
Theosophical Art and Way of Life, 15 December 1911

VIRGINIA SEASE

TEMPLE LODGE

Translated from German by Marguerite V. Miller and Douglas E. Miller

Temple Lodge Publishing
Hillside House,
The Square
Forest Row, RH18 5ES

www.templelodge.com

Published by Temple Lodge 2012

Originally published in German under the title *Rudolf Steiners Versuch einer Stiftung für theosophische Art und Kunst—15. Dezember 1911: Eine Betrachtung nach 100 Jahren* by Verlag am Goetheanum, Dornach, 2012. The Appendix is a translation of 'Ein Esoterisch-Sozialer Zukunftsimpuls. Versuch zur "Stiftung" einer Gesellschaft für theosophische Art und Kunst' from *Zur Geschichte und aus den Inhalten der ersten Abteilung der Esoterischen Schule 1904–1914*, GA 64. Used by kind permission of the Rudolf Steiner Nachlassverwaltung

A catalogue record for this book is available from the British Library

ISBN 978 1 906999 40 7

Cover by Morgan Creative incorporating a portrait of Christian Rosenkreutz

Typeset by DP Photosetting, Neath, West Glamorgan
Printed and bound by Berforts, Herts.

CONTENTS

Preface to the English Edition

The impulse for this publication originated in December 2010 in Spring Valley, New York during a meeting of the North American Collegium of the School for Spiritual Science. This Collegium is composed of representatives who are active in the various Sections working in North America, and it fosters contact with the leaders of the respective Sections at the Goetheanum in Dornach, Switzerland. A request came to me to enter with them into certain aspects of the 15 December 1911 'Endowment for a Theosophical Art and Way of Life', since the following year would mark the centenary of this unusual occurrence connected with Rudolf Steiner's work. After a rather short presentation we engaged in a varied and fruitful exchange of ideas and impressions. This was made possible in large measure because the representative of the Medical Section, Gerald Karnow, MD, had printed his English translation of Rudolf Steiner's address and Marie Steiner's foreword. That little pamphlet served further as the inspiration for the translation of the Endowment address found in this volume.

The mood at the conclusion of our meeting resulted in a suggestion that the author of the present volume should publish her contributions as a study of the 'Endowment for a Theosophical Art and Way of Life' which would be available in time for the centenary of the Endowment impulse in December 2011. When embarking on this task in the autumn of 2011 it became obvious that not only the expository text would need to be translated into English but also the many quotations that were not already available in English. For this reason the only feasible way to have these reflections appear in print by December 2011 was to focus first on a German edition.

This very fine English translation emerges from the cooperative work of Douglas Miller and Marguerite Miller. Marguerite serves as the representative for the Section for Literary Arts and Humanities on the aforementioned Collegium, and had therefore participated in the meeting in December 2010. They both deserve a significant expression of gratitude not only from me but also from the many people for whom English is their mother-tongue or an acquired language.

Virginia Sease
Goetheanum
Dornach, June 2012

PREFACE TO THE GERMAN EDITION

It does not often happen—except perhaps in the realm of natural-scientific research—that an attempt, doomed to failure from the start, is so valued a century later that the goal and circumstances of the attempt are still examined and published. It is rarer still in esoteric-human relationships. But this is exactly the intention of these reflections. For those familiar with the work of Rudolf Steiner (1861–1925) and conversant with the enormity, the diversity and the depth of his writings as well as with his pedagogical, social, medical and other impulses, it may seem strange that an unrealized attempt would be placed here at the centre of these reflections. In addition, a kind of moral question accompanies this: Is it justified to take up something that, in fact, could not be realized? This question occupied the author of this book for a long while—especially during this year when celebrations of the 150th anniversary of Rudolf Steiner's birth are taking place worldwide. Nevertheless, the question repeatedly arose whether this publication might not be able to focus three aspects of the attempt that are relevant for our present time. I will briefly mention these aspects here; later they will be explored more fully. The first is that the Endowment attempt allows us to experience the art of 'interpreting' in the Rosicrucian way. This can create a decisive tone in our relationship to the world. Another is awakening to an understanding of the fact that even the best attempt—even one undertaken by a very lofty individuality—is doomed to be fruitless if not all the participants are able to overcome their personal ambitions. Finally, from our own human-earthly perspective, we cannot predict whether the seeds dormant in the attempt might bring about moments of flowering, of ripening, of fruitfulness in the future. Such thoughts led to this publication.

I am indebted to two persons in particular. This text would have remained in the realm of my personal work if not for the always engaged, competent and positive collaboration of my assistant, Andrea Jeserich, who encouraged me to put these observations into writing; and, in the end, the careful editing of the publisher, Christiane Haid. Similarly my thanks belong to Uwe Werner for his help with acquiring the documentation from the Rudolf Steiner Archive, and to Marc Desaules for the documents concerning the history of the branch in Neuchâtel.

Virginia Sease
Goetheanum
Dornach, November 2011

1 CONCERNING THE YEAR 1911

Examining the events of 1911 from the vantage point of Rudolf Steiner's enormous activity, we can establish that this year stood especially under the sign of the Rosicrucian stream—which means, more specifically, under the sign of the great individuality Christian Rosenkreutz. Particularly during the last third of 1911, Rudolf Steiner revealed mighty, spiritual inspirations in order to make this leader of humanity in the fifth post-Atlantean cultural epoch (AD 1413–3573) accessible to his contemporaries who were striving for an understanding of the spirit within the German Section of the Theosophical Society.

During the previous year, this motif had already emerged and found special emphasis in the title and theme of his first Mystery Drama, *The Portal of Initiation, A Rosicrucian Mystery through Rudolf Steiner*. The Munich Congress at Whitsun 1907[1] as well as the subsequent lecture cycle *The Theosophy of the Rosicrucian*,[2] in which the Rosicrucian path of schooling is described, made it possible for people at that time to prepare themselves inwardly in regard to Rosicrucianism. These events within the German Section of the Theosophical Society formed the basis for the further deepening and new horizons that then appeared in 1910.

The year 1910 stood under the sign of the production of the first Mystery Drama—followed in the summer of 1911 by the second drama, *The Soul's Probation, Life Scenes as a Sequel to the Portal of Initiation through Rudolf Steiner*[3]—but the appearance of the Christ in the etheric world was first and foremost at the centre of Rudolf Steiner's depictions during this year. It was imminent for humanity during the first third of the twentieth century and it awaits us still today. He spoke for the first time about this theme on 12 January 1910, in Stockholm,[4] then in many places throughout Germany, and also in Rome and in Palermo.

At the beginning of 1911 Rudolf Steiner gave the final lecture in the cycle *Okkulte Geschichte, Esoterische Betrachtungen karmischer Zusammenhänge von Persönlichkeiten und Ereignissen der Weltgeschichte* [Occult history, esoteric observations on karmic connections between personalities and events in world history][5] held between 27 December 1910 and 1 January 1911. These lectures made visible various ancient relationships of destiny (Eabani and Gilgamesh) and the last lecture on 1 January ended with special emphasis on the individuality of Novalis. We may view this lecture cycle as a kind of karma preparation—not only for later remarks about karma such as the ones made in the great karma lectures of 1924, but as an everyday, practical preparation for the second Mystery Drama with its retrospectives on the incarnations of the main characters during the Middle Ages. The closing words of this lecture on the first day of 1911 contain something that points to the future of developments yet to unfold:

> Regard what was just said as something that should create a gateway to a feeling for the times. And in a certain way it may be symbolic that we may use a small transition from one segment of time to another in order to permit these ideas that encompass transitions of time to work in our souls.[6]

A 'feeling for the times' is cultivated here based on various incarnations.

The year 1911 began with great promise. Although there are no extant notes for the lecture Rudolf Steiner gave the next day in Stuttgart, it is known that he spoke publicly about the Buddha. A day later, the foundation stone was laid at Landhausstraße 70, which would give the Stuttgart branch its own home. In Rudolf Steiner's address for this occasion he spoke clearly about the meaning of environments created to be appropriate for spiritual work. Unfortunately this lecture is not fully documented. But there is a seed of a thought that most certainly had an inspiring effect on the building association founded at the end of the year:

> We should be clear that as long as we are forced to meet with one another in rooms whose forms belong to a culture in decline our work will have to encounter—to a greater or lesser extent—what is dedicated to decay. The spiritual stream will not be able to establish the new culture it is called to bring until it is granted the ability to work into the purely physical forms—the very walls themselves—that surround us. Spiritual life will have a different effect when it flows forth from rooms [whose] measured proportions [are] determined by spiritual science, [whose] forms arise out of spiritual science.[7]

Following Rudolf Steiner's sojourn in Stuttgart, a significant and grave interruption gave rise to increasing uncertainty during the next several months and brought the work to a virtual standstill. Marie von Sivers—whose work on behalf of every inner and outer aspect of the task was so indispensable—had fallen ill. In a letter to Edouard Schuré dated 31 January 1911, she wrote how she now had to withdraw completely.

> This year I grew more tired than ever before, and ... I [am] ... compelled to keep myself very quiet. I remain in my room and do no work... This is the time when we would be negotiating the theatre

contract for our August performances ... However, as a result of my unfortunate state of health, Herr Steiner has not yet been able to decide about setting the dates. Since there is still much time before August, I continue to hope that it will not become impossible to carry out our plans.[8]

The lengthy duration of the illness is shown in a subsequent letter from Marie von Sivers to Edouard Schuré a half year later, on 1 June 1911. She wrote from Portorose (which was then in Italy):

I would be pleased if the Munich performances could be delayed until September but that will not happen because of the availability of the theatre. I fear that it is still too early for me but I hope the guardian angels will help. If providence permits it, we will have three performances ... Herr Steiner visited the Austrian branches and in between returned here repeatedly for brief periods.[9]

Under discussion were the productions of Edouard Schuré's drama *The Sacred Drama of Eleusis*, a repeat performance of the first of Rudolf Steiner's Mystery Dramas, *The Portal of Initiation*, and *The Soul's Probation*, which Marie von Sivers describes here as 'sequel to the Rosicrucian drama'. We can hardly imagine what it would have meant for the impulses at that time had this closest colleague of Rudolf Steiner's not recovered completely—her collaboration was indispensable not only in the realm of the theatre, but in every facet of the esoteric work. Much of what took place during and after the performances would never have been possible—for example, the event of 15 December 1911 in which she had a most central role.

The architect Carl Schmid-Curtius was able to forge ahead at an astonishing pace with the construction of the Stuttgart branch building so that its dedication could take place on 15 October 1911. Rudolf Steiner gave a long dedicatory address in which he also expressed the hope for executing an even larger building in Munich—since he experienced 'being surrounded by what our Spirit Temple is' as a necessity. In the evening he spoke in detail about the occult meaning of form and colour in the context of an occultism that has a determining effect on daily life. He continued:

There are beings who actually have these forms in the etheric world and when we observe one of these figures, our etheric body adjusts so that through its own movements it creates forms in accord with the lines of the figure. This means it engenders a thought form which now emerges from it. And depending on the thought form, our etheric body will be in a position to enter into a real association with one or the other kind of being. These figures are the mediators through which we are prompted to create in ourselves the thought forms—which means the movement forms—in our ether body.[10]

Rudolf Steiner was already in Stuttgart for the dedication of the building, and he spoke the next day on the theme 'In what sense are we theo-sophists, and in what sense are we Rosicrucians?' We can surmise that this theme was particularly relevant since less than three weeks earlier—at the dedication of the Christian Rosenkreutz Branch in Neuchâtel—Rudolf Steiner had given two very detailed lectures about the life, work and cosmic significance of Christian Rosenkreutz.

On the first of October 1911, he spoke to the Basel [Switzerland] Branch about the Christ Mystery of our time, a Mystery connected to the etherization of the blood.[11] This is not the place to enter into these accounts—the notes of these lectures themselves[12] as well as an abun-dance of study material offer insights into the cosmic significance of Rudolf Steiner's revelations about the past, present, and future of this mighty individuality. Peter Selg examines in detail Rudolf Steiner's own relationship to Christian Rosenkreutz in his book *Rudolf Steiner und Christian Rosenkreutz*.[13] We will come to speak more of Christian Rosenkreutz later in these considerations.

We can find two fundamental aspects of Rosicrucianism in this lecture on 1 October 1911. However, it is important for our consideration of 1911 to touch first upon a challenge connected with the Theosophical Society itself, a challenge that confronted both Rudolf Steiner and the members of the German Section of the Theosophical Society. Annie Besant, then president of the Theosophical Society, resided at the headquarters of the Theosophical Society in Adyar (India). She worked closely with the Englishman Charles Webster Leadbeater (1847–1934) who had become a member of the Theosophical Society in 1883 and had been impressed with Helena Petrovna Blavatsky. He is regarded as the principal initiator of the impulse to found the Order of the Star in the East. Both Annie Besant and Charles Leadbeater believed they had identified the World Teacher—the next incarnation of Christ Jesus—in the Indian youth Jiddu Krishnamurti who was 14 years old at the time. Based on his own research and because of his own spiritual responsibility, Rudolf Steiner was obligated to take a position on this error. How did he do so? Far from acting in a way that could be construed as an attack on the individuals involved, he instead undertook an intensification of his work—presenting verbally and in writing the true nature of the Christ

Being. A few of Rudolf Steiner's statements in the lecture on 16 October 1911 that touch on this theme may serve to bring some clarity and emphasize the significance of the Rosicrucian principle for the further development of anthroposophy. Fundamental to all questions regarding Rosicrucianism is Rudolf Steiner's remark: 'Rosicrucianism flowed into our stream; it will be worked on collaboratively, and also practised to a certain extent.'[14] At that time Rudolf Steiner had not yet spoken—as he would later—about 'our stream' as the one connected with Michael, in the sense of the Michael School and the Michael cultus.[15] As a further indication of the presence of Rosicrucianism, Rudolf Steiner explained:

> We are the Rosicrucians of the twentieth century! For us, there is no other task than to connect with those principles that Rosicrucianism had and to make them applicable to the advancement of theosophy . . . All our strivings are directed towards understanding what sounds so easy: opening the heart to the spiritual world that is always around us; understanding a phrase such as this in the way Christ Jesus spoke it: I am with you always [even] unto the end of the world.[16]

2 THE SITUATION IN THE THEOSOPHICAL SOCIETY BETWEEN 1903 AND 1911

It can be said for various reasons that the first epoch of the Theosophical Society came to an end when Henry Steel Olcott (1832–1907), the co-founder and first president of the Theosophical Society, fell ill and subsequently died in Adyar on 17 February 1907. Probity and respect for his fellow man were among the significant qualities of his being—and they permeated his deeds as well. These character traits were apparent in him early in his life, notably in his work as a lawyer in his homeland, America. Because the 33-year-old Olcott had a reputation for being incorruptible, Edwin M. Stanton, the US Secretary of War, had commissioned him to investigate the assassination of President Abraham Lincoln in 1865. Olcott first encountered Helena Petrovna Blavatsky at a spiritistic/psychic reading in America in 1864; the two of them saw through the deception of those proceedings. Based on this event, Henry Steel Olcott recognized the need to protect the wisdom Helena Blavatsky carried, and also the need to create a society for the dissemination of her insights. Thus the Theosophical Society was founded in the city of New York in 1875.

According to Rudolf Steiner, 'the initiators of Rosicrucian wisdom'[17] were involved at this time—but later other paths were pursued. By 1878 Helena Petrovna Blavatsky and Henry Steel Olcott were living in India. Helena Blavatsky died in England in 1891.

Rudolf Steiner met Olcott in 1903 and held him in high regard. Olcott introduced Rudolf Steiner as the new General Secretary of the German Section of the Theosophical Society at the time. At the third Congress of the Federation of European Sections of the Theosophical Society in June 1906, Rudolf Steiner held a lecture with the title 'Theosophy in Germany 100 Years Ago' in which he spoke about Lessing, Goethe, Novalis, and others. Olcott esteemed both this lecture and Rudolf Steiner's work.[18]

Henry Steel Olcott died on 17 February 1907. The Munich Congress of the European Sections of the Theosophical Society took place at Whitsun—and bore the stamp of Olcott's passing. This gathering was the first opportunity for European theosophists to meet following his death. A speech of appreciation was given by Rudolf Steiner; and Mathilde Scholl wrote a report of it for the *Mitteilungen* [newsletter] in which she described how he [Olcott] '... was possessed of an extraordinary genius for organizing that had been needed in order to give the right direction to the Theosophical Society on the physical plane. However, Olcott's activity

Helena Petrovna Blavatsky

was also valuable because he had in his very being respected the striving of every other human being to develop himself.'[19]

Rudolf Steiner wrote to the members:

> Before his passing, our honoured president and founder circulated ... all manner of correspondence to the general secretaries in which he reported that he received the instruction from the higher worlds that he was to name a certain personality, i.e. Mrs Besant, as his successor. [...he] asserted that certain Masters who are usually known in theo-sophical circles by the names M. and K.H. [Moria and Kuthumi] had appeared to him and had given him these instructions.[20]

> One can have the opinion that Olcott should not have communicated all of this. But this report can likely be attributed to a weakness during his final days of life that were distinguished by a difficult illness. Likewise, the naming of his successor in violation of the by-laws can be attributed to this weakness. The by-laws give him no right to name his successor, only a right to suggest someone.[21]

Blavatsky and Olcott

Despite the confusion surrounding these events, Rudolf Steiner recognized Annie Besant as president. It is astonishing that despite all the later difficulties she was one of the first theosophists to acknowledge Rudolf Steiner's spiritual greatness.[22]

Let us turn our attention once again to the founding of the German Section. Rudolf Steiner, Marie von Sivers and Annie Besant had met one another in London in July 1902; the German Section of the Theosophical Society was founded later that year in October. Thus, Rudolf Steiner had held to the occult law that called for connecting to what already existed in so far as possible. Rudolf Steiner and Marie von Sivers allowed themselves to be accepted into the Esoteric School. Two years later, in 1904, Rudolf Steiner became the Arch-Warden of the Esoteric School in Germany and Austria. In the beginning, Rudolf Steiner and Marie von Sivers held Annie Besant in high regard; on 27 August 1904, Rudolf Steiner wrote to Mathilde Scholl: 'Annie Besant is the messenger of the Masters.'[23] However, by 1905 differences had already begun to emerge. In the esoteric lesson on 20 October 1905, Rudolf Steiner mentions that Annie Besant ought to be more conscious of the fact that other races—and, in this context, the word can mean other streams—are equally justified. In addition, he said that the more the theosophists reached out to her with love, the more effective she could be.[24]

An important step in the work took place in Munich during Whitsun,

1907—through the Congress of the Federation of European Sections of the Theosophical Society. This event was important for the esoteric Christian stream, the stream that Rudolf Steiner identified there as the Rosicrucian stream. This has been elaborated in a richly detailed book published on the occasion of the centenary of the 1907 Munich Congress.[25] In it, various authors explore the most important themes. They demonstrate how, in fact, this congress came to be what Marie Steiner called a 'separation of souls'. The point was that pupils needed to identify themselves as belonging to the Eastern occult path, under the leadership of Annie Besant with the Masters Kuthumi and Moria, or as taking guidance from Rudolf Steiner with Master Christian Rosenkreutz and Master Jesus. The esoteric pupils had to decide whether they wanted to continue on their way with Rudolf Steiner or with Annie Besant. The right to choose in freedom accorded by their teacher signalled a new, significant step in the development of esoteric relationships. It was the practice in esoteric streams of that time—and also earlier—that the pupil was called by the head of the school. In his capacity as the Arch-Warden for Germany, Austria and Switzerland Rudolf Steiner inducted people into the Esoteric School by this process—as did Annie Besant in her role as the leading figure of the school that had its centre in Adyar. A free decision about a pupil's future membership stood entirely outside the practice at that time. Notes made by a pupil in the Esoteric School on 1 June 1907 illustrate the fact that this had now changed:

> But no one should believe there is disharmony among the Masters of the East and the Masters of the West. The Masters always live in harmony ... Until now, both Schools were united in a great circle under the shared leadership of the Masters. Now, however, the Western School has made itself autonomous and henceforth two equal schools exist, the one in the East, the other in the West ... The Eastern School is led by Annie Besant, and anyone who feels in his heart more drawn to her can no longer remain in our school. Each must scrutinize for himself in which direction the longing of his heart leads.[26]

A conversation took place between Rudolf Steiner and Annie Besant during the Munich Congress. Marie von Sivers was present, as well, in order to translate if it became necessary—and for this reason she was a witness to the conversation. Annie Besant remarked that she did not regard herself as competent to speak about matters related to Christianity.[27] On 7 June 1907, immediately upon her return to England, she wrote a letter to a long-time theosophist, Dr Wilhelm Hübbe-Schleiden, who had at first supported Rudolf Steiner and then gradually withdrew from him.

Dr Steiner's occult schooling is very different from ours. He does not know the Eastern path and therefore he is unable to teach it. He teaches the Christian-Rosicrucian path that is helpful for many—but it is different from ours. He has his own school and he carries responsibility for it. I consider him to be a very good teacher of his own direction and find him to be a man with real knowledge. He and I work in complete friendship and harmony but in different directions.[28]

This statement by Annie Besant falls short of the truth; it is a misrepresentation of facts. The situation became increasingly volatile in a similar but more pronounced way during subsequent years and contributed to the separation of the members around Rudolf Steiner in the Theosophical Society and the founding of the Anthroposophical Society in Cologne, Germany on 28 December 1912. The following accounts illustrate the misrepresentations, especially in the example of the General Meeting of 1911.

After the 1907 Congress in Munich, the congresses were to occur every second year; the next one took place in Budapest. Annie Besant and Rudolf Steiner were both present. The newsletter published by Mathilde Scholl for the members of the German Section of the Theosophical Society provides a detailed reporting of the Congress. Rudolf Steiner himself writes a report for the newsletter that includes a summary of Annie Besant's lecture 'The Christ; Who is He?' He notes: 'In this lecture we can see that there is no disharmony but rather harmony between Eastern and Western life—if one is only inclined to see the matter in the right sense.' Rudolf Steiner then refers to his lecture *From Christ to Buddha* that was held immediately before Annie Besant's contribution. In his report for the *Mitteilungen* [newsletter], he points out that the members were able to become increasingly familiar with the Rosicrucian stream through his lectures between 1907 and 1909—although it would be another two years before he took up the great revelations about the individuality of Christian Rosenkreutz in his work with the members. He speaks about

> . . . the three great names . . . within Rosicrucian theosophy referred to as especially deserving of reverence. The three names existed throughout the Middle Ages. They were also known to representatives of a dogmatic church authority who often required of their orthodox adherents a confession in the form of a set expression—a curse: 'I curse *Scythianos*; I curse *Saratas*; I curse the *Buddha*.' During the Middle Ages, these three individualities were cursed when someone wanted to affirm that he was a Christian. Christian Rosicrucianism knows these three figures as lofty light-beings. We will speak later about Scythianos. For

Mathilde Scholl 1908

Western initiation, Saratas is a great teacher—none other than Zarathustra ... He was among the great inspirers of Rosicrucian wisdom. In
the same manner, the Buddha was counted among the great indi-
vidualities. The individual contributions they brought flowed at that
time into a combined contribution for the development of humanity.
Thus the great impulse could be offered that we designate as the
Rosicrucian impulse.[29]

Although the inner circles of the Theosophical Society were made
aware of a certain event before the congress in Budapest, Rudolf Steiner
tried to maintain an outward collaboration with Annie Besant during the
congress. The event concerned the closest colleague of Annie Besant,
Charles Webster Leadbeater, who advanced the claim that the future
World Teacher, the Lord Maitreya, would incarnate in a 14-year-old boy
from Adyar, Jiddu Krishnamurti, whereupon the boy would become a
vessel for the reincarnation of Christ.

In my estimation—from the perspective of a century later—what
ensued during the following years can be counted among the greatest
occult, social and human tragedies after the end of the dark Kali Yuga age.
The subject can be mentioned only briefly here in the context of our
present perspective. In December 1909, Annie Besant admitted the 14-
year-old Krishnamurti into her esoteric school. In March 1913, legal
proceedings were filed against Annie Besant by the father of Jiddu
Krishnamurti and Nityananda, his younger brother. The father was
seeking to bring about the return of his sons. The basis of the suit was the
unwanted attention given to the brothers by their teacher Leadbeater as
well as Annie Besant's exercise of extreme influence over the boys.
During the trial, Annie Besant denied ever having called Jiddu Krishnamurti by the name Alcyone; she further denied that she had claimed he
was or would become the Lord Christ or the Lord Maitreya. Nevertheless, it was established during the trial that an initiation of Krishnamurti
had taken place during January 1910.[30]

In her work *Krishnamurti: 100 Years*, the biographer Evelyne Blau
describes how Annie Besant decreed that '... the first initiation should be
prepared during the nights of January 11 and 12, 1910'. Many years later,
in 1972, Krishnamurti himself described in the third person how this
came about:

This boy was thus prepared, bathed, and carefully clothed ... and led
into Dr. Besant's room [She was not in Adyar that night.—VS]. There
he fell asleep or became unconscious—all these things during those 24
hours or more are not clear to me. And as he returned from this

Besant, Leadbeater, Krishnamurti and Raja in December 1911

condition, everyone noticed … an amazing change in the boy's face. Some fell to their knees before him and touched his feet.[31]

The Order of the Star in the East was founded a year after the reported initiation event, on 11 January 1911. In an appeal to the members of the Theosophical Society later that year, Annie Besant wrote:

Besant and Krishnamurti

The Order of the Star in the East was founded in order to assemble under one roof all those within and outside the Theosophical Society who await the coming of the World Teacher and who would want to share in the wonderful privilege of preparing the way of the Lord ... May the peace of the Masters be with you and their wisdom guide your steps. Your true servant, Annie Besant, President of the Theosophical Society, Adyar, November 1911.[32]

We will come back to November 1911 when we turn our attention to the event at the centre of our considerations.

In his lecture 'Theosophy and Anthroposophy—The History of a Tension-filled Relationship' held on 27 January 2007, Lorenzo Ravagli draws attention to the important fact that on 12 January 1910 Rudolf Steiner was lecturing in Stockholm at 6.30 p.m.—an unusual hour for a lecture—for the first time on the theme of the appearance of Christ in the etheric world. Rudolf Steiner explained that the event would begin to take place in the 1930s. People who are able to perceive this event gain access to a new supersensible revelation of the Christ.[33] Rudolf Steiner spoke about this theme in many places—in Germany, Rome and Palermo, as well as in Oslo in 1910.

At this juncture it is essential to pay due respect to the character of Jiddu Krishnamurti by noting that he himself dissolved the Order on 3 August 1929 during a large assembly of its members at a camp in Ommen, the Netherlands. At the time he was 34 years old and for more than 20 years had experienced the enormous veneration of thousands of people. In his address at the dissolution he describes the basis for his decision:

I maintain that truth is a pathless land, and you cannot approach it by any path whatsoever, by any religion, by any sect. That is my point of view, and I adhere to that absolutely and unconditionally. Truth, being limitless, unconditioned, unapproachable by any path whatsoever, cannot be organized; nor should any organization be formed to lead or to coerce people along any particular path.[34]

Let us return to the beginning of this event. Rudolf Steiner's great work—the development of his Christian-Rosicrucian theosophy—was in no way impaired by the outer reality of the difference between him and Annie Besant and her followers, a situation that had grown increasingly tense. On the contrary, there were around 2000 members of the German Section of the Theosophical Society, and even branches in foreign countries that had affiliated directly with the German Section rather than with Adyar. An example of this is the first group in the United States, the

Krishnamurti in Old Age

Saint Mark's Group in New York (1910). Rudolf Steiner's inner attitude was that in esoteric matters only the positive was effective, not the negative. Thus the commotion surrounding the identification of Krishnamurti as the new World Teacher—even the reincarnation of Christ—was not taken up by Rudolf Steiner, was not pursued by him, but was instead ignored. Rudolf Steiner's positive way of working revealed itself in logical, precise and truth-based presentations of spiritual relationships in lectures, books, the Mystery Dramas, the esoteric lessons with their mantric content, in rituals accompanied by instructional lessons, and in countless private conversations.

No further meetings took place between Annie Besant and Rudolf Steiner after the 1909 Congress. The next congress was to have taken place between 16 and 19 September 1911, in Genoa. In the newsletter, Mathilde Scholl reported a strange incident—and what took place as a result.

> In mid-September the time had arrived for a large part of the lodge leadership and other members to get ready for their trip to the Congress that had been in preparation for a long time. A more or less mystical darkness will likely hover for all time over the reasons the Congress was catapulted into nothingness at the last minute by a telegraphed order—leaving a group of hundreds of theosophical members with the questionable destiny of dealing with a useless trip to Genoa!—Fortunately, tireless efforts by headquarters were successful in informing the majority of the theosophists in time. For those who for whatever reason had already left for Italy, a likely first impression of disappointment was replaced with the surprise of finding Dr Steiner there, and being richly

rewarded in Milan as well as in Lugano and Locarno with lectures given to a small circle. What was unfortunate about the cancelled Congress was mainly that the major efforts by those who had organized the arrangements in Genoa were now in vain, and the organizers were deprived of their well-deserved reward for this work!—Returning home from Italy, Dr Steiner held another series of especially important lectures in various Swiss towns. For all those who had the pleasure of being able to take part, the dedicatory meeting of the 'Christian Rosenkreutz' lodge in Neuchâtel will long be remembered. In the small rooms of Professor and Mrs Petz—rooms that accommodated only a limited number of members and felt all the more intimate as a result—the being and activity of this great occult personality chosen as the guardian spirit of the lodge was spoken about over the course of two evenings. Indications were given about the mighty etheric flowing of forces streaming from Christian Rosenkreutz, forces we call on when we want to pursue theosophy in the right sense without, as a result, wanting to identify ourselves with the Rosicrucianism of times past. Again and again, Dr Steiner emphasized the utterly *central* position of theosophy with its task of letting everything that has entered into human development as spiritual impulses and inspirational forces flow together into a living unity; we have to understand the Mystery of Golgotha stands at the centre of this for all time.—From this lofty vantage point, theosophy can be conscious that something was given to the West with the immortal ether forces of a Christian Rosenkreutz— something connected with a deepened understanding of this Mystery of Golgotha that, even now, as a result, the Eastern approach must do without. Our Western spiritual science thus sees itself entirely disinclined to negate foreign values; it restricts itself to a simple statement of *facts* based on occult research and open to verification by each and every thinking person.[35]

Annie Besant later tried to explain these odd events, asserting that she had not cancelled the congress but only announced that she would be unable to attend.[36]

Rudolf Steiner transformed the negative effect of this situation into a positive one—as he always did. Thus, in the days during which the congress was to have taken place he held lectures in the Italian-speaking Swiss cities of Lugano (17 September), Locarno (19 September) and in Milan (21 September); these lectures likely reflected some of the content he would have brought in Genoa. In the preface to *Der Christus-Impuls im historischen Werdegang* [The Christ-impulse in the course of history], which contains the lectures in Lugano and Locarno, Marie Steiner describes how the Theosophical Society and—in hindsight—likely Annie Besant as well were very troubled by how many members were turning to Rudolf Steiner's esoteric-Christian teaching. Marie Steiner reports how the themes taken up by Rudolf Steiner dealt with Buddhist wisdom and Western Christian esotericism. Thus, in 1947—36 years later—the preface to the lecture cycle just mentioned states:

> They had juxtaposed this content to a Christ Jesus who now had incarnated in the flesh as an Indian boy—according to her [Annie Besant's] teaching. Such a gaping difference yielded no common ground for thoughtful, knowledge-based discussions like those that should have taken place during the congress in Genoa . . . The congress was cancelled at the last minute for inscrutable reasons.[37]

The end result was that Rudolf Steiner could clarify for those present at his three lectures the situation regarding the sphere of the Bodhisattvas, the rank of Buddha, the Christ-individuality during the three-year incarnation from the Baptism in the Jordan to the event on Golgotha, and the appearance of Christ in the etheric world—and how people could prepare themselves for the Reappearance of Christ in the etheric. The three lectures served as clarification of various inadequate or even false understandings and interpretations of spiritual relationships that were being disseminated by the Theosophical Society controlled from Adyar. At the same time, Rudolf Steiner could open even broader vistas to an understanding of the Christ.

As mentioned earlier, these lectures took place on 27 and 28 September 1911, both in Neuchâtel. We can gather from documents of the still-extant branch near Neuchâtel that approximately 20 members heard these lectures.[38] If we want to measure the full meaning and weight of Rudolf Steiner's attempt on 15 December 1911 to endow a Society for a Theosophical Art and Way of life, we must approach the greatness and singularity of the individuality of Christian Rosenkreutz in a mood of solemn earnestness. While Rudolf Steiner had already spoken of Christian Rosenkreutz before the two lectures in Neuchâtel—for example, as the Master of Western Christian esotericism[39]—with these lectures in September 1911 he gave humanity the key to unlock the door to this individuality. If we are able to gain even a small measure of insight into these comprehensive relationships, it is because Rudolf Steiner as interpreter opened up enormous vistas in regard to the spiritual and earthly course of this entelechy's development—its past deeds, its present mission under the sign of the Christian Mystery, and its future activity in connection with the soul-spiritual development of humanity. At the very beginning of his explanations of Rosicrucianism in the lectures given immediately following the Munich Congress of 1907,[40] Rudolf Steiner points to Christian Rosenkreutz without saying more about him. He refers to 'That lofty spiritual individuality who in the outer person of Christian Rosenkreutz entered the physical plane and acted again and again as the leader and teacher of the Rosicrucian stream ...'[41] Further details are given for the first time in the two lectures in Neuchâtel in September 1911, and in the period following when he set forth a great arc to this individuality and shared the most significant details about him.

Even today we can experience Rudolf Steiner's words of greeting on 27 September 1911 as a great riddle. Through what was just discussed we have developed a measure of insight into events just prior to this. Rudolf Steiner's words of greeting point to a possibility, perhaps even an esoteric lawfulness:

> It fills me with a deep satisfaction to be here for the first time in this newly founded branch that carries the lofty name of Christian Rosenkreutz—and thus offers the possibility for me to speak for the first time more specifically about Christian Rosenkreutz. What comprises the Mystery of Christian Rosenkreutz? ... Christian Rosenkreutz is an individuality who is active when incarnated as well as when not embodied in a physical body, an individuality who is active not only as a physical being and by means of physical forces but above all spiritually by means of higher forces.[42]

We have Rudolf Steiner to thank for liberating Christian Rosenkreutz from the prison of the merely legendary, from the slanderous histories that recorded him as a magician, a swindler, as a dubious alchemist. It is incumbent on us today to approach this leader of humanity with an ever-growing understanding.

A brief sketch based on Rudolf Steiner's research results can serve here as historical orientation. The individuality of Christian Rosenkreutz stands in the Cain stream;[43] this means that he has the capacity to apply insight and knowledge in bringing about transformation in the material world. Another known appearance is as Hiram Abiff whose involvement with Solomon and his Temple (frequently dated between 962 and 955 BC) entered the world through Christian Rosenkreutz as the Temple Legend. The Temple Legend portrays how Solomon conceived the idea of the temple while Hiram had to translate the plan into a physical reality. Rudolf Steiner pursues this line further and finds the Hiram individuality incarnated almost a thousand years later in Lazarus, the brother of Martha and Mary Magdalene. With this incarnation, the direct connection to Christ in the earthly world begins.

> The awakening of Lazarus described in the eleventh chapter of the Gospel of John is a process of initiation in which Christ Himself participates as the hierophant during the three and a half days. Christ calls his name: 'Lazarus, come forth.' He addresses his ego being ... Lazarus receives new life from Christ so that through him—'the disciple whom the Lord loved'—the message of the Gospel of John and the Book of Revelation can enter the world. After his initiation by Christ, Lazarus bears the name John ... We can also use the designation 'the disciple whom the Lord loved' as a key to understanding his initiation. The Lord, Christ, sanctified the ether body of Lazarus John, which means that the etheric quality of the Christ also lives in him.[44]

In the more than thousand years that followed, there were quiet incarnations of the individuality of Christian Rosenkreutz that allowed great heart forces to develop. Rudolf Steiner describes in the Neuchâtel lectures how this individuality experienced a further initiation shortly after the middle of the thirteenth century; how as a child he was raised by twelve wise men with great care and under singular circumstances. Rudolf Steiner's choice of words to describe this event is particularly illuminating:

> It was known by this collegium of twelve wise men that in this epoch *a child* [emphasis—VS] would be born who had lived in Palestine at the time of the Christ-event and had been present at the Mystery of Golgotha ... An especially spiritual individuality was embodied in this child.[45]

In the initiation through the twelve wise men the entire wisdom of the seven Atlantean epochs and the five post-Atlantean epochs could be taken up—so that this wisdom could be brought back in a metamorphosed form suitable to our fifth post-Atlantean time period. During his initiation, the youth had an experience like Paul's on the road to Damascus. In the etheric realm of the earth he encounters the Christ in a sheath of light. His astral body is permeated by this light substance and thereby sanctified. For this reason, as Rudolf Steiner describes it, a short time after he awoke from the process of initiation he:

> ... repeated all of the wisdom he had acquired from the twelve ... but in a new form. This new form was as though given by Christ Himself... The twelve called it the true Christianity, the synthesis of all

religions ... The occult process must be imagined in this way—that the fruit of the initiation of the thirteenth has been preserved as the remaining portion of his etheric body within the spiritual atmosphere of the earth. This remaining part works inspirationally on the twelve as well as on their pupil so that the Rosicrucian occult stream can emerge from them. But the activity of this etheric body continues and it then permeates the etheric body of the thirteenth who incarnates once again.[46]

Since that time he has been known esoterically as Christian Rosenkreutz and, after his subsequent incarnation, he also bears this name exoterically.

If we take up Rudolf Steiner's comprehensive descriptions of these macrocosmic-microcosmic secrets time and again, we become ever more reluctant to refer to them in an abbreviated form like this. And yet they are fundamentally essential to these observations. Without them we would never arrive at the vast meaning of the attempt at an Endowment for a Theosophical Art and Way of Life, because the individuality of Christian Rosenkreutz has a central role in this attempt. For this reason, as well as for the sake of completeness, the next incarnation of Christian Rosenkreutz should be mentioned here. He already incarnated again in 1378 and lived a long life until 1484 when he died at the age of 106. This life, too, bears the signature of a Christ-initiation in 1459. Christian Rosenkreutz was 81 years old at the time. According to Rudolf Steiner, a 'lofty emissary of the Christ'—Manes—assisted in this initiation. From this example we can come to understand how one initiate can help another. In this instance, it was through the incorporation of the Christ-ego into the ego organization of Christian Rosenkreutz—which means that ever since then Christian Rosenkreutz has carried a replica of the Christ-ego in his own ego.[47]

A book written at the beginning of the seventeenth century by a young student, Johann Valentin Andreae, and based on an inspiration, describes in symbolic, emblematic images a great sevenfold initiation process. It is entitled *The Chymical Wedding of Christian Rosenkreutz Anno 1459*.[48] This work occupies a singular position in world literature. There are also other texts from this period concerned with the activity of Christian Rosenkreutz and his pupils: *Fama Fraternitatis* (1614) and *Confessio Fraternitatis* (1615). The Rosicrucian brotherhood through which a new culture was to be established can be traced to these writings. The origin of the Rosicrucian brotherhood is situated in the initiation undergone by the individuality of Christian Rosenkreutz in the thirteenth century. Later, this individuality was identified by various names, the most widely known of which was the Count of Saint Germain. Rudolf Steiner notes: 'The Count of Saint Germain in the eighteenth century was the exoteric reincarnation of Christian Rosenkreutz.'[49] Among many other deeds, the Count of Saint Germain sought to prevent the French Revolution through his connections in the French court.[50] According to Rudolf Steiner

> ... at that time [he] represented the view that people must be led in a peaceful way from a worldly culture to the true culture of Christianity... He (Christian Rosenkreutz) appeared in his eighteenth-century incarnation as the guardian of the innermost secrets of the Brazen Sea and the sacred Golden Triangle [an allusion to the Temple Legend and Hiram—VS] with the warning: Humanity must develop gradually.[51]

In the first Neuchâtel lecture (27 September 1911) Rudolf Steiner makes very clear that Christian Rosenkreutz had not just been active in the past. Even today he works for all humanity, providing impulses and formative ideals with a view to making it possible to experience Christ in His appearance in the etheric. He works as well for the individual human being in so far as he is spiritually striving and active. 'If you are able to become an instrument of Christian Rosenkreutz, you can be assured that the least activity of your soul will exist for all eternity.'[52]

3 THE ANNUAL MEETING OF THE GERMAN SECTION OF THE THEOSOPHICAL SOCIETY

On 10 December 1911, the Annual Meeting of the German Section was held in Berlin. It began at 10.15 in the morning and ran late into the evening.

Programme of the Annual Meeting

After the usual formalities of an annual meeting had been attended to (confirmation of voting percentages for the delegates from the various branches; the treasurer's report), a motion was put forward to re-examine and rescind the expulsion of Dr Hugo Vollrath—a decision reached three years earlier at the Annual Meeting on 26 October 1908. Related requests to address the assembly and the ensuing discussion take up 25 pages in the meeting report submitted by Mathilde Scholl. The following citations from the report may offer a small glimpse into the difficult situation surrounding the person of Dr Vollrath. First, however, it must be noted that the expulsion occurred before Dr Vollrath was made responsible for the administration of the Order of the Star in the East by Annie Besant. The founding of this order, as discussed previously, dates back to 1911.

The request to speak submitted by Reverend Klein provides us with a picture of the situation at that time. He put forward a resolution:

> ... I urge you to consider this resolution with the utmost seriousness. By honouring Dr Vollrath through the bestowal of special titles, Adyar has created an impossible situation ... Adyar has to be aware of what took place in 1908. It is incomprehensible that Dr Vollrath has been named secretary of the Order of the Star in the East. Either—Or! When Dr. Vollrath attacks the General Secretary in such a pamphlet and the General Assembly declares itself to be emphatically opposed to this act, such an accolade is inwardly impossible to endorse ... I would like it known in Adyar that we are not disposed to tolerate this, and we experience it as an impairment of our work when Dr Vollrath is supported by Adyar in this unclear way—to put it mildly.

Dr Steiner speaks:

> ... a complete separation of the objective facts from the personal aspect will be easier and clearer for us than it was earlier. The objective element is as follows. At the end of October or the beginning of November, the text you read today was published by Dr Vollrath. This text now exists and is in wide circulation. This text contains a number of things that—were they true—would likely justify even a dog refusing a piece of bread from us ... At approximately the same time, a bulletin appeared from Adyar. In it Dr Hübbe-Schleiden is mentioned as the representative of the Star in the East and Dr Hugo Vollrath as substitute. We, the German Section, are an integral part of the whole Society ... Let us assume that I am personally faced with the question: Will you defend the president? Well!—then someone could say to me: If you do that, aren't you agreeing with the person who wrote this

brochure—because the president names as her agent the person who is so opposed to you? Let us assume that someone then says: You need not accept that response. You can advocate for the president despite the fact that these things are said in the brochure—because the president can, after all, make a mistake. However, because of her duties, the president was thoroughly informed from the outset about what was happening. What had occurred was reported to her from the very beginning with the necessary clarity. The president, nevertheless, set in a motion this vote of no confidence against the General Secretary of the German Section. The necessity of choosing either the one or the other of them is entirely untenable. Mrs Besant must have known the situation. At present, the matter has reached a point where Adyar has placed the General Secretary in a position where it is impossible to defend the president. This is an abnormal situation and I can assure you that I would find almost no alternative more painful . . . But there is one factor that must guide us unconditionally: the absolute adherence to a foundation of truth. I have set myself this one task and I would like to mention it. Those who only know the history of occult movements but not their bases will have an impression of how intimately connected charlatanry and occultism have always been. It is a fundamental occult experience that what separates them is as thin as a single strand of a spider's web. The one thing I can claim is that I have set myself this ideal: it must be demonstrated that an absolute truthfulness and honesty in every detail can be connected with an occult movement. If all we are able to do here were to vanish, the one thing I hope would never disappear is this—there once was a theosophical movement that had as its motto: It must be demonstrated that one can be both a real occultist and a representative of the unvarnished, absolute truth. Anyone familiar with the history of religious movements will agree with me about this . . . The most painful thing is that something like this could occur in our theosophical movement. It is a deep pain for me, more painful than anything else—because I must admit that no one can love Mrs Besant more than I. But this pain is wrested from the truth and the truth is what we hold as the loftiest ideal. However, as the poet says, measured against love, the truth is cruel.

Towards the end of the Annual General Meeting, Rudolf Steiner says:

I want to add that no one has the right to say I said something against the president of the Theosophical Society today. All I have said is that it is impossible for me to defend the president.[53]

4   AN INITIATIVE FOLLOWING THE ANNUAL MEETING OF THE GERMAN SECTION

The report of the General Meeting also contained an announcement entitled 'Federation Founding'. On 14 December 1911, Baron von Walleen (b. 1863, Sweden; d. 1941, Denmark)[54] gave a talk about his 'Experiences on Lecture Tours in Scandinavia and England'.

According to the report of the General Meeting, on the following day (15 December 1911) Baron von Walleen expressed the wish of members who did not live in Germany '... to find a form which would make possible—unhindered by any conflicting influences—the cultivation of spiritual work in the sense of *Rosicrucian spiritual science* [emphasis—VS]'. For this purpose, an independent, free federation would be founded to which people outside Germany could also belong. The next day (16 December 1911), a unanimous decision was reached that also commented on the principles to which the federation wished to dedicate itself:

Baron von Walleen

The founders of the federation trust that the spiritual stream they want to serve has set down such strong roots in so many hearts that the federation may prove to be a suitable framework for this spiritual stream [by which is meant the Rosicrucian stream.] . . . The federation has absolutely nothing to do with the Theosophical Society in either form or content . . .[55]

'Guarantors' were designated who would be responsible for creating working groups where they lived. Among the guarantors in the German-speaking area were: Marie von Sivers, Mathilde Scholl, Sophie Stinde, Countess Kalckreuth, Dr Peipers, Adolf Arenson, and Dr Carl Unger—all of them individuals who shared the experience of another highly significant event on 15 December 1911, the event to which this reflection is dedicated.

In order to correct an assertion that the Anthroposophical Society arose as a result of the federation impulse in 1911, Rudolf Steiner reported ten years later, on 8 April 1921, about the actual circumstances:

. . . that those who already stood within our anthroposophical work . . . founded the Anthroposophical Society quite apart from the founding of this federation. The Society went on to develop further whereas the 'federation' gradually passed from a gentle sleep to we might call a social death.[56]

Rudolf Steiner's further activity in the days before and after the General Meeting

Rudolf Steiner's other activity during these days after 10 December 1911 should also be mentioned for the sake of completeness.

The first general meeting of the Johannes Building Association already had taken place on 12 December 1911; it had been constituted in April of that year and entered in the commercial registry in Munich on 9 May 1911. This building association—given the name Johannes after Johannes Thomasius, the main character in Rudolf Steiner's Mystery Dramas—took on the task of constructing a building in Munich for the Mystery Dramas. Land for the building was even purchased in 1911. However, the municipal authorities were very slow to implement the approval procedure and, in the end, denied the building application. As a result, a parcel of land in Dornach, Switzerland was made available two years later through a gift from the dentist Dr Emil Grosheintz. This gift made it possible to continue the building impulse. Thus, construction could begin

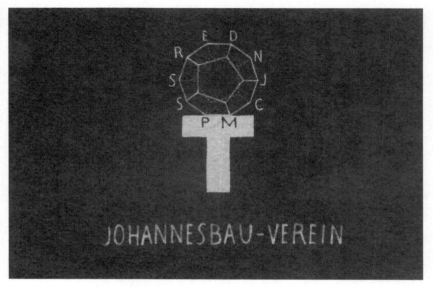

Membership card of the Johannes Building Association

immediately following the rejection in Munich and the laying of the foundation stone in Dornach on 20 September 1913.[57]

Furthermore, on 12, 13, 15 and 16 December 1911, Rudolf Steiner gave lectures on pneumatosophy. Here we must note how insightfully Marie Steiner's 1931 introduction to the first edition of these lectures addresses our theme.[58] In addition, on 14 December 1911, Rudolf Steiner offered a public lecture in the Architektenhaus in Berlin entitled 'The Prophet Elijah in the Light of Spiritual Science'. It was the seventh lecture in a series of 16 lectures that began in October 1911 and ended in March 1912. Rudolf Steiner had himself chosen the titles of these lectures.[59]

The activity surrounding the founding of the 'federation' connected with Baron von Walleen's initiative has already been mentioned. On 17 December 1911, Rudolf Steiner speaks about the 'Relationship of Goethe's *Faust* to Goethe'. Interestingly, Rudolf Steiner spoke as a substitute for Frau Camilla Wandrey who had fallen ill. He begins his presentation with the following thought: '... [I would like to] make a few scattered and more casual remarks about Goethe's *Faust*.'[60] On 19 December 1911, Rudolf Steiner speaks about 'Symbolism and Fantasy with Regard to the Mystery *The Soul's Probation*'. The figure of Capesius and the fairy tale of the rock spring wonder as well as fairy tales in general are of central importance in his remarks. The presentation describes

Design for the Munich Building

various soul-spiritual states in connection with the development of the human being and of language.[61]

The last lecture Rudolf Steiner gave during this period was held on 21 December 1911, in Berlin, and takes up the theme of Christmas: 'Christmas—A Festival of Inspiration'. We can imagine that many people had remained in Berlin after the General Meeting and heard the lectures given by Rudolf Steiner. They were thus able to take into themselves an inner substance as a preparation for the Christmas festival. Those present might well have experienced Rudolf Steiner's explanations as a kind of echo of his earlier address on 15 December 1911 concerning a Society for a Theosophical Art and Way of Life.

> That is our spiritual-scientific ideal—that we can feel ourselves as one with what people of earlier times created, often out of the most hidden depths of souls ... the great festivals attend to this if only we are able to portray for the soul their hieroglyphic meaning inscribed in the script of time through the truths of spiritual-scientific research.[62]

On 16 December 1911, Rudolf Steiner held an esoteric lesson[63] as well as an instructional lesson within the cultic context of the Theosophical Section [in Rudolf Steiner's collected works, this is called the 'cognitive-cultic section'.—VS]. The instruction concerned the difference between Freemasonry and the cognitive-cultic section inaugurated by Rudolf Steiner within the German Section. It was in this lesson that Rudolf

The First Goetheanum, Dornach

Steiner distanced himself decidedly from the designation 'Freemasonry' and explained that the notation 'F.M.' had to be removed. In addition, there was a brief characterization of what the cultic work in the cognitive-cultic section included. He describes this work as a 'Misraim Service' that came down first from the Egyptian Mysteries and was then shaped anew by [the evangelist] Mark, a pupil of Paul. Here Rudolf Steiner offers a kind of definition that was not noted in the stenographic report but survives through reports by some who took part. 'What is performed here is an occult service called the Misraim Service, which is as much as to say: bringing about the union of the earthly with the heavenly, the visible with the invisible.'[64] In an instructional lesson held in Munich on 30 August 1911, Rudolf Steiner had already mentioned that Ormus (an Egyptian initiate) worked with Mark and both were disciples of the Christ after the Mystery of Golgotha and the resurrection. The Mysteries and rituals were re-formed through the efforts of both.

A central aspect of the General Meeting, December 1911

After Baron von Walleen had reported on 14 December 1911 about his experiences abroad, Rudolf Steiner gave an address; in his collected works it has the title 'Why has what has been understood until now as the theosophical movement been represented within the Theosophical Society?'[65] The year 2011 marks the 150th anniversary of Rudolf Steiner's birth; it also marks the centenary of the great milestones in the descriptions of Christian Rosenkreutz that came through Rudolf Steiner. Thus it is important to recall that these descriptions were being offered at the same time the crisis involving the centre in Adyar was taking place within the German Section of the Theosophical Society. This background of the address provides us with deep and far-reaching perspectives o Rudolf Steiner's position and the decisions he reached between 1900 and 1911. These decisions and inner attitudes form the necessary background for what took place the next day, 15 December 1911. At the conclusion of the address on 14 December the next day's event was announced. This can be found in the collected works of Rudolf Steiner as an appendix to the address on 15 December 1911.

In these concluding words, Rudolf Steiner explains not only his position but also his method in regard to these enormous difficulties: '... what is needed is what is positive ... Something positive requires deeds not only at the outset but deeds carried out consistently.' After a further mention of Baron von Walleen's comment '... that—when it exists—the content always creates the framework', Rudolf Steiner continues with his announcement concerning the next day. Even today, it is possible to sense his urgency in the way he formulates his words:

Thus I am taking the liberty of noting something today that I will be obliged to speak to you about tomorrow morning at 11.00 from this room. It is in regard to something that already exists as such, something that was arranged recently under especially solemn circumstances—but in such a way that it should be shared in a quite particular manner. What can be announced along these lines will be made known tomorrow morning. We will see then what is intended.[66]

From Hella Wiesberger's research, we know that in a gathering of the cognitive-cultic work held in Stuttgart on 27 November 1911 Rudolf Steiner spoke to a small number of people about his intention to implement a new way of working.[67] Rudolf Steiner's remarks concerning 'especially solemn circumstances' refer to the cultic institution that was to take a new form on 16 December 1911, the day following the endowment address. This new form was intended to obviate all confusion between Rudolf Steiner's work and that of Freemasonry. In view of its future consequences, this deed of Rudolf Steiner's ought not be undervalued esoterically or exoterically.

5   AN ESOTERIC-SOCIAL IMPULSE FOR THE FUTURE

THE ATTEMPT AT AN 'ENDOWMENT' OF A SOCIETY FOR A
THEOSOPHICAL ART AND WAY OF LIFE

Before we concern ourselves with the Endowment address and some
aspects related to it, it is essential to consider in more depth Marie Steiner's
decision to circulate privately a limited mimeographed printing of her
summary of it during the penultimate year of her life. This selfless deed
belongs among the most central of the many she accomplished on behalf
of Rudolf Steiner's body of work. Because of her pivotal task in this
attempt at an endowment, Marie Steiner figures more prominently than
any of the others who took part. And it is she who afterwards suffered
most as a result of the situation and the relationships that ultimately caused
the Endowment to be regarded only as an 'attempt'. We will be able to
examine these situations and relationships later in the course of these
observations. Her foreword details the reasons why she felt compelled to
publish her summary. At the same time, it conveys a comprehensive
cultural retrospective that comes from her own ripeness of soul, and it is
profoundly Christian. Although a relatively brief summary, it leads the
reader through microcosmic and macrocosmic circumstances as well
through historical-social references—the Church, secret societies, a
begin, she emphasizes how Rudolf Steiner was able to elicit advan
in people through an education in the esoteric so that they would
to take up future tasks as a service to the evolution of huma
mentions in her foreword how 'Rudolf Steiner first spoke a
future tasks ... to a small circle of his pupils and attempted to f
souls on the meaning of those far distant tasks that have to arise
developing human will, free of selfishness.'[68]

We gain some further insight into the gathering on 27 November 191
in Stuttgart when Marie Steiner mentions that Rudolf Steiner later lec-
tured on the same subject before a larger audience on 15 December 1911.
She points out that the December gathering was not part of the General
Meeting of the Theosophical Society, but was held in addition to it. In
her report, she emphasizes the solemn mood in which Rudolf Steiner
formed the assembly. Since Marie Steiner was always at Rudolf Steiner's
side, the way she describes his demeanor can be considered trustworthy.
Although the first part of his address was not recorded verbatim, Marie
Steiner took her own notes. We can emphasize three central points. What

Rudolf Steiner says here stands apart from the content of the General Meeting—it is a 'direct communication from the spiritual world'. It is to be understood as a call to humanity. And there must be a period of waiting to determine whether something will resound as an echo from humanity. She notes the possibility for such a call to be sounded three times. And she notes as well that if the call finds no resonance in humanity after the third time it sounds, it will not be able to draw near again for a long time. The second call, as it were, took place through Rudolf Steiner on 15 December 1911, as well as slightly earlier with a few of his pupils (on 27 November 1911).

After this introduction by Marie Steiner, we read Rudolf Steiner's words as they were assembled from Marie Steiner's notes and the shorthand notes of Berta Reebstein-Lehmann. Berta Reebstein-Lehmann had been a member in Berlin since 1905; she became Marie Steiner's secretary in 1909. Following her marriage to Otto Reebstein in 1916 she moved to Stuttgart in 1920. She cared for the Stuttgart branch building at Landhausstraße 70 until the couple moved to Dornach in 1930. After Otto Reebstein died in 1944, Berta Reebstein-Lehmann resumed her task as secretary to Marie Steiner—during the last four years of Marie Steiner's life.[69] Even this brief outline of Berta Reebstein-Lehmann's biography demonstrates that the notes of the Endowment address available to Marie Steiner were from someone with whom she was very familiar and in whom she placed her confidence. Only much later—in 1984—was it possible to add the notes made by Mieta Pyle-Waller, which Rudolf Steiner had actually reviewed, as well as notes by Elizabeth Vreede and the shorthand record by Franz Seiler. It is important that these personalities be noted since we can be certain that they were present and participated even though they were not mentioned in connection with any specific task within the Endowment on 15 December 1911.

Rudolf Steiner opened the gathering with words of welcome to those present; then he begins his remarks with a clarification of the situation he is to address: 'It must be emphasized, however, that what will be said now has absolutely no connection to what has happened earlier in this General Meeting; nor is it related in any way to earlier proceedings.'[70] This statement notwithstanding, if we wish to come to an understanding of the esoteric import and potential effects of this attempt at an endowment, it is essential to trace in detail the events preceding it. The history of the attempt will serve to illuminate other important matters as well.

Following Marie Steiner's mimeographed circulation of the proceedings in 1947, members of the Anthroposophical Society only gradually became aware of what it described. Even then, when people took note of the Endowment, they often did not know quite how to consider it in the context of Rudolf Steiner's body of work. To a certain extent, this is also the case today. Knowledge of the publication arrived rather quickly in America by way of the actor Hans Pusch (1902–76). In 1926 Marie Steiner had asked Hans Pusch to play the part of Theodosius in the Sun Temple in Rudolf Steiner's Mystery Drama; in 1932, she then entrusted him with the role of Johannes Thomasius, which he played until he left Dornach and emigrated to America in 1939. In 1932 Hans Pusch married Ruth Barnett, a young eurythmist from America. As someone in whom Marie Steiner placed enormous trust, Hans Pusch soon received a copy of the private publication. In my view, she could not have put this text into the hands of a more appropriate person in America. Throughout their years in America, Hans and Ruth Pusch interpreted the impulse for speech formation, the Mystery Dramas, eurythmy and anthroposophy as a whole in a lofty, cultural and spiritual way.[71]

Turning our attention now to the record of this Endowment address, we might ask what approach will bring us closest to an understanding of it. Some of it proves to be puzzling; the implications of other parts are almost overwhelmingly sublime. In addition, questions arise about specific situations belonging to the larger historical picture of Rosicrucianism. Although we have to deal with a record that is compiled from various notes, there is nevertheless a coherence to the content and style that can lead the reader logically to an utterly new experience. Therefore I prefer a path that more closely follows the text but also allows for the introduction of various explanations from additional sources. For this reason, the full text of the address is appended at the end of this volume. Some aspects will be examined only briefly if their scope proves to be too extensive for this reflection.

The starting point of Rudolf Steiner's presentation is his explanation of
the complex conditions necessary for the representation of ideals, and of
how the requirement of an 'absolute and unqualified acknowledgement'
is inwardly related to this representation. This is the case with '... what all
the world has striven for in bringing people together—in societies,
associations ...'[72] While Rudolf Steiner does not wish to raise doubts
about the 'validity' of such a 'bringing together', he does intend to add
something to what already exists. In this connection, however, he alerts us
to a danger: 'that an assertion of belief in something may no longer be
valid when this assertion of belief is given expression ... [that there is] the
potential danger of becoming untruthful by merely expressing something'.[73] He then offers the example of someone saying, 'I am silent.'
Here the thought becomes untrue when it is expressed, and the possibility
exists '... that a verbal expression of belief in something may be inherently self-contradictory'.[74] Rudolf Steiner asks that the example be
'... understood in the sense of Rosicrucian principles that have existed
since the thirteenth century'.[75] How are we to understand Rudolf
Steiner's request? The phrase 'Rosicrucian spiritual science' was used in
Baron von Walleen's description of founding a federation—which offers
evidence that the members of the Esoteric School who participated in the
attempt at an endowment were fully informed about Rosicrucian principles. This might lead us towards a provisional interpretation.

    We know that the three basic pillars of Rosicrucianism are truth,
beauty and strength—accompanied by the principle of development in
the sense of metamorphosis. Rudolf Steiner's mention of Rosicrucian
principles alludes to the possibility of forming an affiliation that cannot
arise if its foundations are untrue, that is if they are derived from the
sensory world. The sole true possibility is that the foundations for such an
affiliation have their home in the supersensible world. In view of this,
Rudolf Steiner notes a necessity 'connected with more recent occultism';
for us, that also means Rudolf Steiner's occultism—'... representing
certain aspects of this occultism, bringing them to the attention of the
world ... for the immediate future'.[76] It is a call with an important
stipulation—something new had to be attempted that has nothing to do
with organizations and societies. We can well imagine how this stipulation may have moved the hearts of those present after they had endured

such difficult exchanges in the annual meeting, and had experienced the devastating remarks made by Rudolf Steiner in his address on 14 December 1911. But it would be wrong to believe that those events were responsible for what Rudolf Steiner intended now. We have already seen that three weeks earlier a small group had met in a solemn mood to receive the new impulse from him. Now, on 15 December he describes how the new impulse is 'something born entirely out of the spirit of that occultism we speak of so often in our circles [Rosicrucian occultism—VS].'[77] This principle of Rosicrucian occultism is as follows: Everything belonging to the supersensible world is taken to be a reality since the sensory world must be understood as a 'replica of the supersensible world'.

Following this brief but meaningful orientation comes the *crucial sentence*: 'Thus an attempt will be made, the kind of attempt that must be made out of the supersensible world—an attempt made not to found, but to *endow* [emphasis—VS] an association of people.' It had not been possible to accomplish this earlier because the difference between founding and endowing had not been understood: 'Thus those spiritual powers that are placed before you under the *symbolum* [emphasis—VS] of the Rose Cross looked away from the attempts to carry this difference out into the world.' Now Rudolf Steiner would make the attempt not to found but to *endow* an affiliation. If the attempt—this second call—is unsuccessful it will be postponed.

What was to be endowed? A way of working! And here Rudolf Steiner makes what he calls 'an announcement'—an expression he rarely uses. Who should undertake this way of working?—'... those who will find themselves appropriately a part of it'. Furthermore, '... this way of working has as its direct origin that individuality whom we in the West have designated for aeons with the name Christian Rosenkreutz'.[78] In order to deepen his characterization for those present, Rudolf Steiner adds a further announcement:

> The first point I have to communicate to you is this: what will enter into life will be a way of working under the immediate protectorate of the individuality whom we designate with the name he has had in the outside world for two incarnations ... It can be characterized—for the time being, for the immediate future—by the provisional name *Society for a Theosophical Art and Way of Life*.[79]

The members who had been present during the lectures in Neuchâtel on 27 and 28 September 1911 already had a comprehensive picture of the individuality of Christian Rosenkreutz—if not before these lectures, then certainly after. Now they had to bring this substance into direct connection with what they were hearing in the Endowment address—which would assuredly have had a strong effect on them personally. For the members at the time, Rudolf Steiner's descriptions were not literature, not a lecture, but a reality in which they participated directly. In the Esoteric School as in the ritual work—in the Misraim Service that Rudolf Steiner later renamed the Michael Service (1913)—it was the responsibility of the members to remain absolutely silent about what took place. Thus for decades the situation of the Endowment as well as how it was related to Christian Rosenkreutz was simply kept secret, kept hidden.

Here we might consider what 'endowing' means outside the context of the Rosicrucian stream. Normally 'to endow' is used as a verb or 'endowment' as a noun. And we associate this with the meaning, the thought and the gesture of giving: a charitable endowment, an institutional endowment, an ecclesiastical endowment. As a verb, the word also acquires a temporal dimension—mostly with historical overtones. In a Rosicrucian context, we find a few indications in Rudolf Steiner's work that suggest 'endow' has a special meaning. Several examples in Rudolf Steiner's work before 1911 might be of interest here as points of comparison. Speaking about the Temple Legend in an early lecture in Berlin on 4 November 1904, Rudolf Steiner establishes quite succinctly and clearly the identity of the being of Christian Rosenkreutz and the Count of Saint Germain. This connection has already been mentioned but now a world historical dimension stands in the foreground: 'Before the French Revolution, a personality who gave warning by predicting all of the important scenes of the revolution appeared to Madame Adhémar, a member of Queen Marie Antoinette's court. It was the Count of Saint Germain, the same personality who, in an earlier incarnation, had endowed the Rosicrucian Order.'[80]

During February and March 1907—before the Whitsun conference in Munich that year—Rudolf Steiner refers to Christian Rosenkreutz and the endowment impulse in lectures that describe the formative principle of Rosicrucianism: 'Rosicrucianism is *one way* of being initiated. It was endowed through Christian Rosenkreutz.'[81] Four weeks later, in a public lecture held at the Architektenhaus in Berlin, Rudolf Steiner speaks on the theme, 'Who are the Rosicrucians?' At the outset, it is his intention to differentiate, to separate Rosicrucianism from the negative perceptions that claim it is charlatanry, making gold from lead, a swindle. Then he begins to develop the actual theme: [He is speaking before an audience that would not have understood 'endowment' in this context.—VS]: 'The historical aspect need no longer concern us except for the fact that we discover from it that Rosicrucianism is a foundation, an endowment that has actually existed in the West since the fourteenth century and goes back to one individual ... *Christian Rosenkreutz*.'[82] The lecture cycle 'The Theosophy of the Rosicrucian' took place between 22 May 22 and 6 June 1907, immediately after the congress. Several weeks later, in Kassel, Rudolf Steiner would continue to elaborate the Rosicrucian theme in connection with theosophy. As an introduction to this theme he says: 'By 1459, a loftier spiritual individuality—known as Christian Rosenkreutz in the outer world—had endowed an esoteric school for the cultivation of wisdom ...'[83] With these few indications we arrive at some insight into the connection between the principle of endowment and the individuality of Christian Rosenkreutz. This is how he works. As a lofty individuality initiated three times by Christ, he gifts, he gives something that has the greatest possible significance for the evolution of humanity. But it must also be possible for such a sublime gift to be received by people—often people who were called—with a fully awake consciousness, with dignity and selflessness, since the gift also comes with a responsibility. This responsibility can only be agreed to in freedom, never by force. It can only be fulfilled in freedom. Thus we have the words by Rudolf Steiner that have already been cited: '... this is the kind of attempt that must be made out of the supersensible world: an attempt made not to found, but to endow an association of people'.[84] In the passages cited from Rudolf Steiner's earlier lectures, we learn that Christian Rosenkreutz 'endowed the Order of the Rosicrucians', that 'Rosicrucianism' means a way of initiation that was endowed by Christian Rosenkreutz, and also that Christian Rosenkreutz worked with a few people to endow an 'esoteric school for the cultivation of wisdom'. In the foreword to her summary, Marie Steiner indicates that the preparation (27 November 1911) and then the event on 15 December 1911 signify a second call, a 'direct communication from the spiritual world'. Implicit in this is that Rudolf Steiner heard the call, the communication, and it was his responsibility to transmit the communication to a circle of his pupils. Thus he worked in very close connection with Christian Rosenkreutz. For years Rudolf Steiner and his pupils had prepared the way for this moment—especially, as indicated, during 1911.

The spiritual task for the modern age, the age of the Michael regency, the age following the end of the Kali Yuga—which is also our age—is as follows:

> ... that a way of working will be endowed among those who will find themselves appropriately a part of it. The nature of the Endowment lets us recognize that this way of working has its direct point of origin in

that individuality whom we in the West have designated for aeons with the name Christian Rosenkreutz.[85]

Shortly before he made this statement in his address, Rudolf Steiner referred to the need to represent certain elements stemming from Rosicrucian occultism and carry them into the world. Describing the way of working in greater detail now, he indicates more precisely that it had *already* become possible to endow something based on a 'branch of this Endowment—namely, the artistic representation of Rosicrucian occultism'.[86] A careful consideration of this situation would suggest that the Endowment itself already exists but has to find further expression at that time through certain people with specific tasks. Rudolf Steiner then uses a provisional characterization to expand upon Christian Rosenkreutz's relationship to the Endowment and its way of working:

> ... what will enter into life will be a way of working under the immediate protectorate of the individuality whom we designate with the name he has had in the outside world for two incarnations—this way of working will enter the world as an endowment under the protectorate of Christian Rosenkreutz. It can be characterized—for the time being, for the immediate future—by the provisional name *Society for a Theosophical Art and Way of Life*.[87]

Here Rudolf Steiner once again mentions that when the requisite preparations have been made and the Endowment enters the world, its name will likewise become apparent.

Rudolf Steiner begins by intentionally setting aside 'a theosophical way of life' since it is 'still entirely in a germinal state', and an understanding for it must still be acquired. However, the situation is completely different for 'a theosophical art'. Rudolf Steiner's joy in what had already been achieved in the arts is perceptible even in the extant notes. In them, he mentions the performances of his dramas in Munich as modest attempts; viewed from the perspective of today, however, they are monumental breakthroughs in the artistic and esoteric realms. In this context he also mentions the artistically designed branch building for the work in Stuttgart as well as the founding of the Johannes Building Association.

What is asked for in connection with the task of the Endowment is a 'spiritual way of working'. Only the person who is able 'to place his own forces in service to what is positive about it'[88] may become a member of the working circle. It was probably a somewhat startling experience for the members who were hearing for the first time during the gathering on 15 December 1911 that something had already happened within the

Endowment 'based on purely occult principles'; a small group had already
been formed [27 November 1911] and had accepted a responsibility in
order to make possible '. . . a beginning for this Endowment so that what
our spiritual stream is might be separated from me [Rudolf Steiner] in a
certain sense and the Endowment provided with an existence (substance)
based in itself—an existence founded in itself!'[89] Rudolf Steiner affirmed
this statement when he emphasized that the small circle had received a
sanction:

> . . . by virtue of its *own* [emphasis—VS] acknowledgement of our
> spiritual stream; in a certain way, it sees the principle of the sovereignty
> of spiritual striving, the principle of federalism, and the independence
> of all spiritual striving as an absolute necessity for the spiritual future—
> and it is to carry this into humanity in the way it finds appropriate. Thus
> within the endowment under consideration *I myself* [emphasis—VS]
> will serve solely as the interpreter of the principles which, as such, are
> only present in the spiritual world—the interpreter of what is to be said
> in this way about the matter's underlying intentions.[90]

How are we to grasp this powerful intention of Rudolf Steiner that was
already so clear to him and to the spiritual world that he could communicate it so decisively? People who have been familiar with this
'attempt at an Endowment' for a long time naturally have worked out for
themselves various ways of thinking about it. In my view, the restrained
sense of tact that generally accompanies this questioning is to be wel-
comed, since it suggests that we need to take into account who is really
qualified to interpret Rudolf Steiner's motivation. Further, if someone
does exist who could do so, would he feel it is his place to make such a
claim? Since we cannot avoid the matter entirely, however—it belongs to
the picture of Rudolf Steiner's life and work—we can mention a few
exoteric circumstances that may be significant. The situation in the
Theosophical Society—already outlined earlier in these observations—
might be compared to a sinking ship; the strong egotism that had mostly
remained hidden behind a façade among the participants now surfaced,
and certain individuals wanted only to rescue themselves and their personal eccentricities, their personal peculiarities. This was the situation in
1911. And the events that took place before the General Meeting—for
example, the founding of the Order of the Star in the East; the Vollrath
case; Annie Besant's attitude that bordered on untruthfulness; the sudden
cancellation of the congress in Genoa—surely all these things would have
spoken volumes to Rudolf Steiner. During this whole period, however,
what he had done and what he had accomplished in the world was

entirely positive and so immense that it is impossible to summarize. Nevertheless, he saw that his task as General Secretary of the German Section of the Theosophical Society was not yet complete, even though he recognized with increasing clarity the impossibility of somehow harmonizing the theosophical movement—which he understood to be a spiritual movement—with the Theosophical Society. Just before the end of his address at the General Meeting of the German Section on 14 December 1911, he spoke about this situation:

> ... among those individuals who are leaders of our theosophical *movement* [emphasis—VS], the opinion exists that the *Society* [emphasis—VS] should be maintained as long as possible. And that is what makes it difficult for me to recommend any direct initiative that would lead in some way to a dissolution of the Society ... that with this Society we have something that resulted—not through us, because we had no part in it but merely came across it—from the founding of the theosophical movement of the modern time. So that the dissolution of the Society as such is certainly not the right thing to do at this time; instead, what is right is what is positive.[91]

Between December 1911 and December 1912, the members of the German Section acted independently within the Theosophical Society, calling into existence their own Anthroposophical Society that had no connection to Adyar. Documents and letters about this can be found in the *Mitteilungen für die Mitglieder der Deutschen Sektion der Theosophischen Gesellschaft (1905–1913)* [Newsletter for members of the German section of the Theosophical Society (1905–1913)] published by Mathilde Scholl in a form that demonstrates in all clarity the relevance and urgency of what was happening at that time.

Three significant facts acquire a place of pivotal importance through Rudolf Steiner's announcement that he would be active in the Endowment only as the interpreter of its principles—principles that exist in the spiritual world. First, as a result of their spiritual-meditative work with him, the small group of Rudolf Steiner's esoteric pupils has become mature enough to work esoterically and exoterically into the outer world. Second, while Rudolf Steiner will support his pupils in the intentions of the work, their efforts in the Endowment are under the protectorate of Christian Rosenkreutz. This should, however, not be interpreted to mean that they will be accompanied by Christian Rosenkreutz in physical form as is sometimes claimed. Third, henceforth what takes place in the Theosophical Society can have no effect on the Endowment because it is entirely independent of that Society. As a result of these three factors, the

Endowment has to acquire a certain form and shape since there are only tasks and duties, 'no honours, no high rank'.

Rudolf Steiner now begins the distribution of tasks, and Marie von Sivers receives the principal task. Here Rudolf Steiner's choice of words is both significant and meaningful. Since Marie von Sivers and four other participants took notes, we can be sure that Rudolf Steiner's words have been accurately reported:

> ... a curator will first be appointed for the external nurturing of this Endowment ... Thus Fräulein von Sivers will be recognized as curator by the Endowment itself. This recognition is nothing other than a recognition interpreted from the Endowment itself; there are no appointments, only interpretations. Fräulein von Sivers is interpreted as the curator of the Endowment. And her task ... will be to do what can be done in the sense of this Endowment in order to solicit (gather) a circle of members appropriate for it—not in an external sense but so that the Endowment will allow individuals to approach it who possess the earnest will to collaborate in this way of working.[92]

This description provides evidence of certain powerful facts: The Endowment is under the protectorate of Christian Rosenkreutz, and Marie von Sivers is recognized as curator by the Endowment itself—thus by Christian Rosenkreutz. This carries with it a very lofty recognition—or what might be considered an extremely elevated degree. She is the sole curator while Rudolf Steiner presents himself as only the interpreter of the principles. Marie von Sivers also held a high position within the ritual work. In it, the altar in the East represents wisdom. Her place was on the left side of the altar in the East; and, as Master, Rudolf Steiner stood on the right side of the altar.[93]

Rudolf Steiner then briefly describes additional tasks and the individuals who would be responsible for them. The structure Rudolf Steiner establishes for the Endowment is often seen as analogous to the structure of the School for Spiritual Science—the General Anthroposophical Section at the School's heart surrounded by the 'professional Sections'.

In his outline of the arrangement for the Endowment Rudolf Steiner portrays an image of a branch for which Marie von Sivers is curator—this can be understood as the main branch. Within it, there will be 'a number of ancillary branches' with their own tasks and led by 'individuals who have been tested within our spiritual movement'. These interpretations include an archdeacon for each individual branch. It is certainly understandable that Rudolf Steiner would want to use terms that were not already burdened or claimed by existing brotherhoods, societies or

Marie von Sivers 1908

organizations. Archdeacon comes from the Latin *archidiaconus*, and is part of ecclesiastical vocabulary. The English word 'archdeacon' can be used in either an ecclesiastical or academic context.

In all brevity, Rudolf Steiner now speaks the names of the personalities and their tasks as leaders of the ancillary branches. He also uses an interesting turn of phrase when he announces that the personality and the ancillary branch had already been 'published' in the small circle. Of course, this does not mean they were published in print as might be understand today; instead it draws on the original Latin *publicare* or medieval English *publish*—meaning that something is made known. Here, however, an opposite principle is evident: the work of these archdeacons is already well known to Rudolf Steiner and he 'interprets' the person and the work. The following individuals and their tasks were interpreted by him for the role of archdeacon: Fräulein Imme von Eckardtstein for art in general; Dr Felix Peipers for the art of architecture; Herr Adolf Arenson for the art of music; Herr Hermann Linde for painting; and Marie von Sivers is also 'published' as provisional archdeacon for literature in addition to her overarching responsibility as curator.[94]

Because the tasks do not arise as a carryover from other, existing relationships, Rudolf Steiner explains in precise detail a further central task—the need for 'someone to watch over this collegial collaboration'.

> ... it will be necessary for a collegial collaboration to be accomplished among those who belong to this way of working; this collaboration will have to occur in a completely different way than has been the case up to now in other (customary) organizations. And we will need (have to have) someone whose task it is to watch over this activity. The role of conservator is being created to watch over this collegial collaboration; this office will be carried by Fräulein Sophie Stinde ... If the way of collaboration—in other words, the principle of organization—is to be achieved, is to appear in the world, we will need a seal conservator. Fräulein [Alice] Sprengel was published as the seal conservator, while Dr Carl Unger will be the secretary.[95]

A consideration of the personalities involved can serve as orientation for our further discussions of the Endowment. Thus we will now turn our attention to brief biographical sketches of them before returning to further aspects of the Endowment address itself.

7 BIOGRAPHICAL SKETCHES OF THE INDIVIDUALS INTERPRETED BY RUDOLF STEINER

Alice Sprengel

Of the eight tasks described by Rudolf Steiner in his Endowment address, that of seal conservator remains the most veiled. Rudolf Steiner introduces this special task given to Alice Sprengel as follows: 'If the way of collaboration—in other words, the principle of organization—is to be achieved, is to appear in the world, we will need a seal conservator. Fräulein Sprengel was published as the seal conservator . . .'

Let us begin by looking at what is known of Alice Sprengel's biography—then at the meaning of her task as keeper of the seal and at the reasons she was responsible for the fact the Endowment for a Theosophical Art and Way of Life remained only an attempt. Finally, her situation during 1914 and 1915 will be described.

From an outline of Alice Sprengel's life by Hella Wiesberger and Ulla Trapp, we know that her youth was painfully difficult. Traces of her youthful experiences were still evident as a soul impression when she became a member of the Theosophical Society in Munich during the summer of 1902. After Rudolf Steiner became General Secretary, she joined the German Section around 1904. She was unemployed when she surfaced in Munich at that time. In 1907, Marie von Sivers invited her to participate in the festival productions during the Munich Congress; by 1910, Alice Sprengel would play the role of Theodora in the Mystery Dramas. Marie von Sivers also took it upon herself to ask among the members about financial help for Alice Sprengel.[96] Alice Sprengel was working in the arts at the time, and Rudolf Steiner himself also helped her by commissioning her to design jewellery of a symbolic nature.

In a letter dated 26 May 1907, Marie Steiner wrote to Edouard Schuré, author of the festival play *The Sacred Drama of Eleusis,* about the performance during the 1907 Munich Congress, which he had not attended.

I did not dare invite you to attend because if the performance [of the Eleusis play] had been a failure, you would have experienced painful moments and undertaken a long, difficult journey only to be met with unpleasant impressions. And then we really did not know until the last moment whether we would be able to go ahead with it [because of various difficulties, most notably because one actress went 'insane' and had to be institutionalized.—VS] . . . After much hesitation, we decided to attempt it with a very impoverished young girl [Alice Sprengel] who has an extremely difficult life and, for want of energy, gives the impression of hopelessness in moments of depression. At those moments she sits down, puts her hands in her lap, and says, 'I just can't make myself do it.' Fortunately, she could 'make herself do' the role of Persephone. That was our concern. Then we saw the spark ignite that had been dormant in her, and every day she grew happier. Her voice, which had been weak at first and always slid down into her chest, became stronger with each day, but it was not until the final weeks that we could be sure people would be able to understand her. To this day, this young girl is completely transfigured and still has the charms of a princess. These days were probably the most beautiful days of her life.[97]

Wilfried Hammacher also cites Max Gumbel-Seiling's description of Alice Sprengel during the production of the Mystery Dramas in Munich: 'The actress who played Theodora was a sensitive person with a quiet voice; she looked so girlish and friendly in her light blond wig and her bright garment with its large rounded collar.'[98]

In his history of the Order of the Golden Dawn, Ellic Howe mentions Alice Sprengel's birth and death dates and also provides further biographical details. It seems there were even two Fräulein Sprengels. *Anna* Sprengel, who is thought to have died in 1893, also has an interesting destiny, but she is entirely unrelated to *Alice* Sprengel. Some years afterwards, Harry Collison, later General Secretary of the Anthroposophical Society in Great Britain, posed a question to Edouard Schuré that pertains to our discussion because it relates to the further destiny of Alice Sprengel. On August 8, 1921, Schuré wrote about this to a Mr Landrieux:

I have known a certain Mlle Sprengel, supposed to have been a member of the Anthroposophical Society of Dr. Steiner and who performed as Persephone in my drama *Eleusis* between 1908 and 1912, a drama which was performed by this society under the direction of Dr. Steiner, and later as Theodora [a clairvoyante] in a mystic drama by the same Doctor. I heard later that this person (who had a theatrical talent of no mean order) had left the Society at the time Dr. Steiner married Mlle de Sivers [24 December 1914] because they said Mlle Sprengel was hoping, so it was said, to marry the Doctor . . .[99]

In his book, Ellic Howe notes that many years later (1957) a question about Alice Sprengel was put to Dr Heinrich Wendt, a judge in the courts

Group photo in Söcking near Starnberg. Alice Sprengel is on the far left

in Mannheim, by Gerald Yorke. Yorke wrote the foreword to Howe's book and had made many documents from his private collection of the Order of the Golden Dawn available to him. The answer from Dr Wendt read:

Alice Sprengel (b. September 28, 1871; d. Bern, Switzerland, 1949) was the illegitimate daughter of a nobleman and the daughter of a Lutheran pastor from Pomerania. To avoid a scandal the mother went to Scotland, and the child [Alice] was born there. In her youth she [Alice] lived in South Shields in Yorkshire. She then returned to Berlin. There she was active in theosophical circles and became acquainted with Rudolf Steiner.[100]

Ellic Howe notes further that around 1915 Alice Sprengel became Theodor Reuss's secretary,[101] and was later engaged on behalf of his activities in the O.T.O (Ordo Templi Orientis).[102]

According to Dr Wendt, she was later (1917) with Reuss in his colony, Monte Verità in Ascona; and in 1937 she became leader of an O.T.O lodge in Locarno.[103]

A better understanding of the traditional background for the office that Alice Sprengel was to have in the Endowment can be reached by outlining a few aspects of this function based on its earlier context in Freemasonry. As already mentioned, beginning in 1906 Rudolf Steiner conducted cultic work in collaboration with Marie von Sivers, at first under the name FM or Freemasonry. Although FM had used the forms of many Freemason rituals, the contents were created purely out of Rudolf Steiner's own capacities. In Freemasonry, all important documents are provided with a seal that certifies the authenticity of the document. In the tradition of Freemasonry, documents lacking a seal are invalid, and in some cases several seals are even necessary. There are different seals, depending on the lodge and the Masonic brotherhood or stream. Freemasons who use seals as part of their work often have a keeper of the seal, which represents an important office reflecting an extraordinary trust-worthiness. Not every system or stream has the office of keeper of the seal. In many lodges, the keeper of the seal is also the archivist. According to Kenneth Mackenzie, such a dual responsibility is especially prevalent in the higher degrees of French Freemasonry.[104] Here we see a more physical use of the seal in a traditional esoteric context. In the case of the Endowment there may well have been an intention to design a special physical seal since Alice Sprengel had some experience in making fine jewellery. Other signs, however, point to a less exoteric function for this office.

Between 1910 and 1913, the members were able to experience the art of Rudolf Steiner's brilliant seal designs in the seals created for the Mystery Dramas. An attentive immersion in them reveals the two aspects of a seal: to keep something secret, to keep it sealed; or to unseal something, to reveal it. In this connection, the Book of Revelation provides us with a universal example. Rudolf Steiner often spoke extensively about it, and he himself made sketches of the seven seals. The seven seals occupied a prominent place in the arrangement of the hall for the 1907 Munich Congress.[105]

The history of seals in human cultures and religions is significant and wide-ranging. To begin, we will consider a few representative aspects of the enormous breadth of 'the culture of seals'. The culture of seals develops over a long period of time. It begins at the time of the Sumerians with rolling seals dedicated to religious themes, and continues with the Egyptians who also associated a great, manifold and legendary tradition with seals and amulets that represent a secret meaning and magical power—like the scarab. Manfred Lurker describes how the word *seal* comes from the Latin *sigittam* and is derived from a diminutive form of *signum* (sign).[106] The use of seals is found in the Old Testament where the seal can be understood as the symbol of 'belonging to God'. But the seal is used more often in the New Testament, for example in the Gospel of John 6:27, 'Labour not for the meat that perisheth, but for that meat which endureth unto everlasting life, which the Son of man shall give unto you: For Him hath God the father sealed.' Additionally, in the first Epistle of Paul to the Corinthians, 9:2, 'If I be not an apostle unto others, yet doubtless I am to you: for the seal of mine apostleship are ye in the Lord.' In Revelation 9:4—in connection with that seventh seal—we hear that those people are to be harmed who do not bear 'the seal of God in their foreheads'.

Here it is possible to mention only a few of Rudolf Steiner's statements about seals to indicate his deep insight into this realm of sphragistics; his statements make evident why the keeper of the seal has such an important office to guard. The closing lecture in the great cycle *The East in the Light of the West, The Children of Lucifer and the Brothers of Christ* was given by Rudolf Steiner on 23–31 August 1909 in Munich during the international summer conference of the Theosophical Society. In it he explicitly uses the expression 'keeper of the seal' in a particular way. On 22 August 1909, one day prior to the beginning of this cycle, Edouard Schuré's drama *The Children of Lucifer* had premiered. Marie Steiner had translated it from French into German, and Rudolf Steiner had rendered it in free verse. In his lecture on 31 August 1909, Rudolf Steiner speaks

The seals provided by Rudolf Steiner for the Four Mystery Dramas

about the great initiates Scythianos, Gautama Buddha, Zarathustra and Manes—in that order. He says the following about Gautama Buddha: 'Thus that being who then went further East as a teacher was, so to speak, already in an advanced position. He was a second great teacher, a *second* [emphasis—VS] great keeper of the seal of the wisdom of mankind . . .'[107] Of course, in this case the meaning is quite far removed from a physical object, and it offers us an opportunity to assess the lofty quality of this cosmic task as well as the significance of the keeper of the seal in the sense of the Endowment.

Rudolf Steiner uses the same terminology two years later—in 1911. This underscores for us the importance of understanding the situation and the real task of the keeper of the seal, Alice Sprengel. It may be helpful to mention here that in the Endowment address Rudolf Steiner speaks of the 'seal conservator' (*Siegel-Konservator*). Following the address, Rudolf Steiner returns to 'keeper of the seal' *(Siegelbewahrer)*, using the masculine form of the German word—with one meaningful exception to be mentioned later. It is noteworthy that Alice Sprengel also uses this term in its masculine form when referring to the office.

The explicit reference to the leaders of humanity in this connection lends a special dimension to the office of keeper of the seal that is significant for our discussion. Rudolf Steiner notes that these initiates are always present in the Rosicrucian Mysteries:

> The individualities of Scythianos, Buddha and Zarathustra were always active in the Rosicrucian Mysteries. They were the teachers in the schools of the Rose Cross, teachers who gave their wisdom as a gift to the earth because the Christ was to be comprehended in His essence through this wisdom. Thus in all the spiritual schooling of the Rosicrucians these ancient initiates who *kept* the ancient wisdom of Atlantis were looked up to with deepest reverence.[108]

The Endowment of 1911 would have stood under the protectorate of Christian Rosenkreutz; in fact, it was already under his protectorate when Rudolf Steiner gave the address in December because he mentions what had been endowed earlier, and indicates that it '. . . relates only to a part of

Alice Sprengel as Theodora

this Endowment ... to one department, to one branch of this Endowment—namely the artistic representation of Rosicrucian occultism.'[109]

When we look more deeply at the task of the keeper of the seal, Rudolf Steiner's words about the exoteric and the esoteric also take on a particular significance. Originally, the two belong together and were only gradually arranged into a duality according to the lawfulness of the Mysteries: '... and if we speak exoterically and esoterically, they are like two different dialects of an inexpressible language.'[110]

It has already been mentioned that Alice Sprengel played the role of Theodora in Rudolf Steiner's Mystery Dramas. As we come to understand why the Endowment for a Theosophical Art and Way of Life remained only an attempt, it is astonishing to realize that Alice Sprengel continued to have a part in the third (1912) and fourth (1913) Dramas. The specific crisis that had begun around the end of 1911—at the latest—did not come to a head until 1914. It remains an open question whether she knew why Rudolf Steiner had not returned to the theme of the Endowment by 6 January 1912.

Rudolf Steiner gives detailed stage directions for the eighth scene in the *Soul's Awakening* (the fourth Mystery Drama); it was to elicit a certain image in the audience member: After the scrim rises, one sees

> ... everything prepared for the initiation of the neophyte who is thought of as an earlier incarnation of Maria. On one side of the sacrificial altar stands the chief hierophant who is thought of as an earlier incarnation of Benedictus; on the other side of the altar is the keeper of the word, an earlier incarnation of Hilarius Gottgetreu; *somewhat* in front of the altar is the keeper of the seal, an earlier incarnation of Theodora ...[111]

Two characters and their tasks are characterized by the word 'keeper'—namely the keeper of the word and the keeper of the seal.[112] We know from various descriptions by Rudolf Steiner that the words as well as the rituals of the temple service had to be maintained in strictest secrecy. The duty to keep silent was a very serious law—so serious, in fact, that a sentence of death was imposed if this law were violated. In the ritual it is a matter of going through the sacrificial steps, the various tests, connected with the elements and the ethers. The keeper of the seal explains the meaning connected with the sacrificial level; thus the candidate for initiation takes shape as a flame:

> We cleanse for thee the form of thine own being!
> Know thou our work; or thou must lose thyself
> within the cosmic ocean formlessly.[113]

The task of the keeper of the seal includes the warning that the candidate for initiation ought not dissolve in 'cosmic ocean', which points to the cosmic chemical element, the chemical ether. Now there is a further interpretation through the keeper of the seal.

The Mystic speaks:

So speaks the one who guards the temple's seal;
feel in thyself the brightening power of wisdom.[114]

The keeper of the seal gives another warning after the representative of the water element has given the neophyte an extensive orientation about the transformation of illusion into being in the presence of the 'fire's flaming power', the 'cosmic ocean' and the 'sounding of the spheres'. Here the keeper of the seal must clearly indicate the consequences of any aberration:

We shape for thee the form of thine own being.
Know thou our work; or thou must lose thyself
as formless being in the cosmic fire.[115]

During this Egyptian initiation scene from the *Soul's Awakening*, we can sense in these few but serious admonitions that the keeper of the seal is the keeper of an important inner secret of the temple, one connected with the levels of sacrifice. The other participants in the temple service have already successfully passed through these levels—which are also to be understood as tests. As mentioned earlier, the seal closes the ritual but at the same time it opens the secret. In the Egyptian temple, the keeper of the seal protects the moment in which the secret can be opened and, on the other hand, warns against failure of the initiation process—it is like a double task. In addition, there is the fact that the *way* the secret was opened was strictly guarded and protected. The betrayal of the Old Mysteries does not just mean the betrayal of their contents, the information; equally serious was the betrayal of the way, the process. The contents had to be conveyed in a certain way depending on the developmental level of the candidate for initiation, his cultural context, as well as the overall needs of the age.

There is a key phrase in the Endowment address that points to the Mystery tradition: 'Fräulein Sprengel was published as the conservator of the seal ...'[116] Here, as elesewhere, Rudolf Steiner uses the word 'published', a term that includes various nuances: to make something accessible, to make something known, to declare something, to announce something publicly. As noted earlier, the word is derived from Latin and has been part of the English language since the Middle Ages. A contrast to 'published' arises in the Endowment address when a different, more central office is introduced: 'The role of conservator is being created to watch over this collegial collaboration; this office will be given to Fräulein Sophie Stinde.'[117] One position is 'created' as an office while others are 'published'. 'Published' can be understood in the following way—that not everything about a particular situation is made immediately apparent. Rather, 'published' indicates that what is considered appropriate for a particular moment in time is made known.

When we consider the other situations in which offices in the Endowment are also 'published' they have something in common that is absent in the case of Alice Sprengel. Rudolf Steiner describes the other people as 'individuals who have been tested within our spiritual movement'. He himself identifies the reason for his choice: 'At the outset, this too is an interpretation and in this way the office of leading such an individual ancillary branch is delegated to a particular person. An archdeacon will be interpreted for each of these ancillary branches.'[118] In the theosophical sense, these interpretations by Rudolf Steiner meant a recognition of each person with regard to what each had accomplished in his or her own field over the years. Thus these individuals had already been 'tested' in their professional work. In contrast, the description of Alice Sprengel's task is *not* based on earlier accomplishments—at least Rudolf Steiner makes no explicit reference to such accomplishments—but is internal to the Endowment itself. The same applies to the office of conservator given to Sophie Stinde as the overseer of the collegial collaboration and the 'way the affiliation is achieved'.[119] To be sure, the difference between this and the calling of Alice Sprengel can be found in that fact that Sophie Stinde was widely recognized and over the years had achieved enormous internal and organizational successes on behalf of the Munich Drama productions. She also took care of the building in Munich and had a tremendous aptitude for bringing various personalities together in constructive working relationships. On the other hand, if we look at what little is known about the development of Alice Sprengel, a somewhat burdened life path emerges. And yet her task is to be intimately connected to that of the overseer of the affiliation, Sophie Stinde: 'If the way of collaboration—in other words, the principle of organization—is to be achieved, is to appear in the world, we will need a seal conservator. Fräulein Sprengel was published as the conservator of the seal ...'[120] In view of this we might ask with a certain justification why Alice Sprengel was later designated keeper of the seal rather than seal conservator, the term used in the record. Is this merely a question of translation? Rudolf Steiner himself came to refer to her as the keeper of the seal after certain conflicts arose. We will return to these difficulties later in our considerations.

Another aspect will be mentioned here, one that Uwe Werner, former archivist at the Goetheanum, found in his research and has kindly permitted me to cite. In a letter dated 28 October 1929, Imme von Eckardtstein—who had been interpreted by Rudolf Steiner as the Endowment's archdeacon for 'theosophical art in general'—wrote that on the solemn occasion of the ME (Mystica Eterna) in Stuttgart on 27 November 1911 Alice Sprengel was designated not as keeper of the seal but as archdeacon for the art of making fine jewellery. Uwe Werner mentions that Marie Steiner had apparently perceived 'an inner connection between the two tasks'.[121] This is probably a correct assumption. There is also the fact that when Marie Steiner first published the text of the 1911 Endowment in 1947 she had at her disposal her own notes and those of Berta Reebstein-Lehmann. Later the notes of Elisabeth Vreede, Franz Seiler and Mieta Pyler-Waller surfaced; Rudolf Steiner himself had read through Mieta Pyler-Waller's notes and had made some corrections.[122] Marie Steiner mentions only the seal conservator; she says nothing of an archdeacon for the art of fine jewellery making. In the conflicts that arose during 1914–15, Rudolf Steiner refers only to the keeper of the seal—as does Alice Sprengel, which corresponds to the role of Theodora that she had played. The art of fine jewellery making was no longer mentioned in this connection.

If we now turn to the others who were to assume responsibility, we can arrive at a fuller picture of Rudolf Steiner's intention for the Endowment's way of working. There are many biographical studies of Marie Steiner-von Sivers. A large amount of her correspondence—especially with Rudolf Steiner—is available to us, as are her forewords to editions of Rudolf Steiner's works, Executive Council documents, and the personal recollections of actors who worked with her artistically. However, the information about the other 'tested' personalities is much more sparse. Some aspects about each person who was to have a role in the Endowment will be mentioned here. In this regard, the biographies Florian Roder published in the Goetheanum's newsletter for members of the Anthroposophical Society on the occasion of the centenary of the Munich Congress (1907—2007) are especially informative.

Sophie Stinde

Florian Roder describes the artistic development of Sophie Stinde (1853–1915) as a painter as well as her remarkable capacity for organization. She also became the chairperson of the Building Association—a further sig-

Sophie Stinde

nificant impulse of the Endowment that arose at the same time. Here we can observe the wisdom that went into 'interpreting' her as the conservator, as the overseer of the way of affiliating in the Endowment. The cultural impulse and the art of organization were united in her in a remarkable way.[123] At her cremation in Ulm (Germany) on 22 November 1915, Rudolf Steiner held a long and moving address that began and ended with a mantra. One week later, in Munich, he delivered a memorial address for her that also included a mantra; and he spoke about her again on 26 December 1915, in Dornach. The cremation address has a particular tone that also offers insight into the constellation of people who had been prepared to hear this second call from the spiritual world and to provide an echo in their future work:

> Our dear friend was by nature someone in whom the Christ could become alive so that she was able to perceive the Christ impulse in the very details of what human labour and human power call forth in the evolution of the earth ... Thus she stood, uniting her striving with this, uplifting those of us who were able to work creatively at her side.

She was also closely connected with the Goetheanum building, and

Rudolf Steiner refers to this fact during the cremation address in a particular way:

> The building that arose in the south to become the sheath for our undertaking was also born from the soul of Sophie Stinde. Not merely through its intention but through that power of love from which alone it could arise—that artistic sense without which a world view is unable to pour forth into art. What we could have only in her—that is what Sophie Stinde brought to us when she came into our midst.[124]

Dr Felix Peipers

The physician Felix Peipers (1873—1944) was interpreted by Rudolf Steiner for the task of archdeacon for architecture within the Endowment. He was an early esoteric pupil of Rudolf Steiner. Florian Roder characterizes Dr Peiper's talents as multi-faceted:

> Early on he sensed his own artistic leanings ... Had he followed his own inner inclinations he would have become an actor; he also fos-

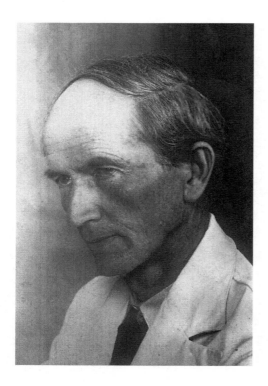

Dr Felix Peipers, MD

tered a strong interest in ecclesiastical architecture ... In the end, he stayed with the study of medicine. His name will forever be connected to an impulse for a new colour therapy ... Coming out of the far distant Mystery past, penetrating academic thought forms, this priestly doctor pressed on to his life's task—learning to apply colours as a new instrument of healing.[125]

Imme von Eckardtstein

We have already noted that Imme von Eckardtstein (1871–1930), was 'published' in the small circle as the archdeacon for general theosophical art in recognition of her achievements in this field. In an obituary for her, Marie Steiner describes how she had been a colleague in the esoteric work since 1904. When the drama work began, she made the costumes:

> With a deep knowledge of historical, cultural documentation, symbolic content and occult realities—and with an enthusiastic love for her task—she set to work ... Her ability to grasp Rudolf Steiner's artistic

Imme von Eckardtstein

intentions quickly was especially gratifying to him. He had only to indicate something and she understood and carried it out![126]

Imme von Eckardtstein felt a particular connection to the scenes of Egyptian initiation in the fourth Mystery Drama, and sketched large and detailed pictures for the costume design. Marie Steiner continues in her obituary:

> Strange, that on this day when she left us the scenes of the Egyptian initiation were presented to the public for the first time at the Goetheanum ... It was like a memorial for her—she who still lingered with us spiritually. She had reflected on these scenes and worked on them so much—and loved them. And the words of that act of initiation could accompany her spirit as it was departing the earth. What she had loved she was able to hear.[127]

Thus in the interpreting of tasks we see the formative artistic impulse present in the very first steps taken by this small circle. The responsibilities encompass theosophical art in general with Imme von Eckardtstein, and the art of architecture with Dr Felix Peipers; they also included the art of painting with the archdeacon Hermann Linde.

Hermann Linde

Each time Rudolf Steiner spoke the name of Hermann Linde he added the words 'our friend'. Hermann Linde (1863–1923) met Rudolf Steiner in Munich in 1904. At the time he was already a well-known, award-winning painter whose works of art were on display in major German museums. In 1909 he painted the majority of the scenery for Edouard Schuré's drama *The Children of Lucifer*, and between 1910 and 1913 the scenery for Rudolf Steiner's Mystery Dramas.[128] We can find the most intimate access to those who had been associated with Rudolf Steiner and his impulses in the words of remembrance he offered them after they had died. After Hermann Linde's death, Rudolf Steiner spoke of him in such detail and with such love that today—almost 90 years later—we can still see this exceptional human being standing before the eyes of our spirit. He describes the times:

> ... when—among those who worked on the Mystery Dramas in Munich—he was one of the most effective, devoted colleagues, one of the most willing to make sacrifices ... When we were working on the Dramas, nothing would have been achieved without Hermann Linde.[129]

Hermann Linde

In his remembrance, Rudolf Steiner also draws attention to Hermann Linde's work on the building: 'He was so permeated with inner love for the work that, in the last years, he connected his whole being with this building . . .' And, as a result, the fire that took the Goetheanum affected him deeply: 'He had to stand among those who were to see what had been created with love and devotion vanish suddenly into ruins . . . during this earth existence, this broke his heart.'[130]

Adolf Arenson

The art of music also was represented by a 'tested personality' from Rudolf Steiner's closest circle. Adolf Arenson (1855–1936) and Sophie Stinde were the oldest among the eight people who comprised the original inner circle of the Endowment attempt. Ronald Templeton has succinctly and sensitively summarized Adolf Arenson's rich and varied biography and his utter devotion to anthroposophy and the Anthroposophical Society.[131]

As a delegate from the Stuttgart lodge to the General Meeting of the

Adolf Arenson

Theosophical Society, Adolf Arenson met Rudolf Steiner in Berlin in 1903. Early in his life he had trained as a businessman but his great love was always music. Between 1873 and 1885, he worked successfully in a family concern in Santiago, Chile—but continued to train as a musician. He married his young cousin Deborah Piza during a brief visit to Hamburg in 1882. Three years later he and his wife returned to Germany and some years later they moved to Bad Cannstatt near Stuttgart. As a composer, he received special recognition for his operas. After joining the Theosophical Society, he became a member of the German Section in December 1902. From that time on, his musical talent and inspiration were devoted to his anthroposophical (at the time, theosophical) work. When Rudolf Steiner inaugurated his Esoteric School in 1904, Adolf Arenson became a member; after 1906, he was active as the leader of this group in Stuttgart. Adolf Arenson served as a member of the Executive Council of the German Section of the Theosophical Society from 1906 until 1913 when the Anthroposophical Society was being founded.

In 1909 Adolph Arenson composed the music for Edouard Schuré's *The Children of Lucifer*; and in 1910, when the first Mystery Drama, *The Portal of Initiation*, was to be produced, Rudolf Steiner asked Adolf

Arenson to compose the music for it as well as for the remaining Dramas. Those who had the good fortune to experience the Mystery Dramas accompanied by Arenson's music could experience how memorable its rich tonality is—that was certainly the case for this author. The temple music especially gives the impression that Adolf Arenson entered into this world very deeply and comprehensively in a soul-spiritual way.[132]

Adolf Arenson dedicated himself energetically to the study of Rudolf Steiner's spiritual science. Thus, in addition to his other writings on various themes, his principal work arose, *Leitfaden durch 50 Vortragszyklen Rudolf Steiners* [A guide through 50 lecture cycles by Rudolf Steiner], and appeared in print in 1930. Even today, this work serves as an orientation to various themes in Rudolf Steiner's lectures.

Dr Carl Unger

Rudolf Steiner 'interpreted' Dr Carl Unger (1878–1929) as secretary for the Endowment for a Theosophical Art and Way of Life. Carl Unger was also Adolf Arenson's friend and co-worker—and was 23 years his junior.

Dr Carl Unger

In a certain way, Carl Unger 'interpreted' Rudolf Steiner when they first met in 1904.

My first encounter with Rudolf Steiner took place in 1904 during a business trip to Berlin [Unger was a mechanical engineer.—VS]. I was to seek out the General Secretary of the German Section, Dr Steiner, on behalf of the group (in Stuttgart) in order to make a mild fuss about not hearing anything from the Section. At that point, I had not read a single line by Rudolf Steiner [What had been printed at that time was limited to Rudolf Steiner's written works.—VS]. During this first conversation, Dr Steiner was very quiet but he directed me to Fräulein Marie von Sivers who pointed out to Dr Steiner the need to begin the long-planned lecture tour now that the book [*Theosophy*.—VS] was finished. Fräulein von Sivers invited me to Rudolf Steiner's lecture that evening. The lecture dealt with the passage from the credo 'suffered under Pontius Pilate'. In an instant, this lecture presented me with the tangible conviction that before me stood a man to whose work I should dedicate my life. The strongest impression was: Here stands *someone who sees* and *someone who knows*.[133]

In the same year, Carl Unger became a member of the Esoteric School led by Rudolf Steiner. Carl Unger dedicated himself to anthroposophy and the interests of the Anthroposophical Society throughout his entire life—until 4 January 1929 when, just before he was to give a lecture, he was shot and killed by a mentally ill man. Renatus Ziegler's comprehensive article about the biography and work of Carl Unger[134] mentions that his career always allowed him to remain financially independent in his professional life and thus free to support Rudolf Steiner's work through personal and official involvements. Renatus Ziegler also draws attention to a remark by Rudolf Steiner in a lecture in Stuttgart on 17 August 1908; it points to Carl Unger's contributions to epistemology:

[You will] sense that there is great benefit when intentions surface within the Anthroposophical Society that strive towards an elaboration of epistemological principles in the best of all epistemological senses. And since we have a worker of extraordinary significance in this realm (Dr Carl Unger) right here in Stuttgart, this is to be viewed as a beneficial stream within our movement.[135]

As with the other members who were asked by Rudolf Steiner to take part in the attempt to endow a Society for a Theosophical Art and Way of

Life, this very brief biographical sketch of Carl Unger can help to provide us with a picture of the mood in which the original seed for the great spiritual initiative was to have been formed. In their inner bearing and their outer activity, all those who took part were representatives of an esoteric activity in life and in art, representatives whom Rudolf Steiner valued as urgently necessary for the period following the end of the Kali Yuga.

In addition to the eight people who had been interpreted in the solemn meeting on 27 November 1911 in Stuttgart and were then mentioned by Rudolf Steiner in this regard on 15 December 1911, we know from Uwe Werner's research that others were present on 27 November as well. In his address, Rudolf Steiner speaks of a tiny circle. It is not known with certainty who else took part on 15 December 1911—with the exception of the four people whose notes have surfaced: Elisabeth Vreede, Franz Seiler, Mieta Pyler-Waller, and Berta Reebstein-Lehmann (whose stenographic notes Marie Steiner was able to consult). We also know for a fact that Rudolf Steiner had read through the notes of Mieta Pyler-Waller. Responsible personalities from the Esoteric School and the cultic work would certainly have taken part in the extraordinary gathering announced by Rudolf Steiner on 14 December and held on 15 December 1911. One thinks here of Maud and Eugen Künstler from Cologne, Michael Bauer from Nürnberg, Albrecht Wilhem Sellin from Munich, Clara Smitz from Düsseldorf, Elise Wolfram from Leipzig, or Alfons Walleen-Bornemann from Denmark.[136]

It is possible to assume with some degree of certainty that Günther Wagner was also present on 15 December. He had been a participant since the early days of Rudolf Steiner's theosophical work. In fact, he had been in Berlin for the first General Meeting of the German Section on 18 October 1903. Rudolf Steiner had written a letter to him on 24 December 1903, which contained esoteric material and four meditative lines—'rendered in the German language from the symbolic emblematic language'.[137] We can assume from this that he was already one of Rudolf Steiner's advanced esoteric pupils—even before the Esoteric School was inaugurated under the leadership of Rudolf Steiner in 1904. Günther Wagner also took part in the cultic work. Shortly after 15 December 1911—on 6 March 1912—Günther Wagner celebrated his seventieth birthday. He was born in 1842, and Rudolf Steiner called him 'our senior'. This celebration took place in the context of the cultic work, and his daughter Ida Koch made notes of it afterwards. Since the mimeographed document is not readily available it is included here.

The 70th Birthday of Günther Wagner
Berlin, 6 March 1912

(Notes made by Ida Koch)

Father sits on a chair bedecked with roses and greens; Gretchen, Paula and I sit next to him.

One to seven strikes of the hammer at the beginning and end, otherwise always seven instead of the usual three. Prayer, etc. as usual.

'I know that I speak for the hearts and feelings of all when I direct these first words to our dear brother, Günther Wagner.' Mantric lines are read:

> The soul's earthly pilgrimage
> It leads to steep mountain peaks
> Where speak the jagged stones of life
> There words are nothing other
> Than riddles alone and questions
> That awaken longing powerfully:
> Only in mountain huts of soul
> Where spirit mood quietly reigns
> When solution beckons to the riddles
> And peace to longing's powers
> Do spirit fruits ripen
> To seeds for eternity.
>
> In your life's pilgrimage—
> Guiding spirit eye—
> These words appear to me
> As the sign of your being.

'I knew weeks ago that such an intimate celebration would surely take place today—but I did not know what I would say until this morning when I opened my heart to the Masters of Wisdom and Harmony of Feelings in order to ask from them a blessing for our dear brother, Günther Wagner. Before I describe what was seen there, I know that I am one with you, my dear brothers and sisters, in expressing the love and loyalty we have for our dear and loyal brother, Günther Wagner.'

Dr Steiner emphasizes how father advised and helped every person who came to him seeking solace, strength and courage—always with the same love and loyalty shown by his soul as it sought and created harmony everywhere; how he had radiated into the world as love everything he had achieved during a long and active life that has always sought the truth;

how he had consecrated his power to the stream of our Theosophical Society; Dr Steiner recalls with pleasure the many moments when he could be close to father—etc., etc.

What came to Dr Steiner from the wise Masters of the East when he opened his heart meditatively to them this morning was not directly clothed in words—rather more like images, indirect images, so to speak. In a community like the one assembled here, he could relate what he was now about to say.

First, images appeared from which still others arose. Dr Steiner then saw a member of the Benedictine Order surrounded by other members of the same order; these were the abbot (Sinnibald) and the elders of this order's cloister. They sat together, not devoted to exercises or other instruction but rather in discussion of more personal thoughts—which rarely happened. And the abbot—who led this order in 1227—told his elders about his father—how he had been very close to him, how this father had gone with the leader of the Third Crusade to Palestine; he related how this father had told of the strains and how he had endured privations and suffering, how he had fought. But the father had also told of life in the Orient as well as how glass was made, for example, and how purple dye was fabricated.—And these stories of life in the Orient and its character made an enormous impression on the boy as he listened—even more than the stories of battle. The father of the abbot also spoke about how he and his fellow soldiers felt strongly that what Friedrich Barbarossa did in the Crusade had a deeper significance than outer events would suggest. The father, who was a Johannine knight (?), was present when the body of the red-bearded emperor was pulled from the River Saleph, and he knew that even though the three parts of his body were buried in Tyrus, in Antioch, and in Tarsus—the birthplace of Paul—his soul had nevertheless flown back to Europe. The father had been a Johannine knight and the abbot had always retained a great affection for this and for the Teutonic knights—although his uncle (the brother of his father?) was opposed to this order.

During his theological studies, the abbot often thought about whether ideas exist *post facto*—the Aristotelean idea—or whether the idea exists *a priori*—as Plato said. He entered the Benedictine Order with the help of old family connections, and was destined to play a leading role in it from the beginning.

It was rare that the abbot and his elders entered into such a personal discussion while they were engaged in the exercises undertaken from four in the morning until sunset; pondering what they had just heard, all the elders left in a contemplative mood. The abbot sat alone for a long while and considered what had just been said. And as he thought back over the course of the conversation, its meditative course, with an expression of tenderness and love, an eight-year-old boy in the habit of the Benedictine Order approached him. Perhaps the abbot's tender gaze inspired the boy to ask a question that might be called nothing less than brash.—The image is rendered here with very strong emotion.—This eight-year-old boy in the habit of the Benedictine Order said to the abbot: 'Your reverence, I am unable to form a conception of God.'—The abbot looked tenderly at the boy who spoke so impudently; he did not answer but instead left without saying a word. And only when the abbot was far enough away that the boy could no longer hear him did he say as though to himself, 'A long time still must pass until we are able to form a correct conception of God.'

'My dear sisters and brothers, this is what came to me when I turned to the wise Masters of the East asking blessing for our dear brother, Günther Wagner. We can, each of us, think what we will about this, based on our own individual leanings. Given the tenderness of the gaze in the image, the person who related this has no doubt about the identity of the abbot. When such things are told, you should not accept them on faith; one can make his own observations. But the one who relates this image is, as already noted, completely sure and certain about the person of the abbot.'

With the Rosicrucian ending, Rudolf Steiner laid three red roses next to the container of consecrated water etc. and passed the censer several extra times over the same at the end. Then he said: 'Now our dear sister, Helene Lehmann, will bring these three roses to our dear brother, Günther Wagner, as a sign of our love and fidelity.'

And then, at the very end, when Dr Steiner had removed this container and was once again passing by the place where father sat, he gave father a kiss on each cheek.[138]

According to Rudolf Steiner's description, a special attempt had to be made 'not to found but to endow an association of people'.[139] Rudolf Steiner's disappointment that his attempt years earlier to describe this difference had not been understood demonstrates how seriously he took this need and how much he valued it. Hella Wiesberger, who prepared the Endowment address in 1984 for the Rudolf Steiner *Gesamtausgabe* [collected works], refers to a statement Rudolf Steiner made on 22 October 1905; it may help us to understand the actual intention of an endowment—other than in the usual sense of a foundation:

> Only when we have formed a society [formed, not founded—VS] whose members are deeply moved by a spiritual power like the one that lived earlier in Christianity, and like the one that still lives as a yearning in the best Christian souls—a power that can be re-won— only then will we once again have a spiritual culture. And such a culture will again engender artists in every domain of life. If you allow theosophy to live in human souls, it will stream forth from souls again as style, as art . . . If the spiritual is lived today in such a society, the world can again serve as an outer expression for it. In this sense the Theo-sophical Society may be able to serve in shaping the culture to come. When we are gathered, we must be clear about the fact that we are the cells who must affiliate with one another in order to form a future culture.[140]

We can note how similar Rudolf Steiner's words are six years later when he describes what he wants to inaugurate with the Endowment: '. . . [people] are unable to affiliate with one another in regard to what they cherish most unless their affiliation is based in the supersensible world and not in the sensory world'.[141] Further, in describing the position of conservator—Sophie Stinde's task—Rudolf Steiner indicates that it is a matter of 'a collegial collaboration to be accomplished among those who belong to this way of working'.[142] Sophie Stinde will watch over the collegial collaboration.

The fact that the difference between endowing and founding had not been grasped in 1905 brought significant consequences: 'Thus those spiritual powers that are placed before you under the *symbolum* of the Rose Cross looked away from the attempts to carry this difference out into the world.'[143] Rudolf Steiner sounds an urgent warning that this

time an association must be successfully *endowed* rather than founded—
otherwise the possibility will vanish for a long time. We can imagine that
if the people around Rudolf Steiner in 1905 had been in a position to
understand this difference, he might have been able to shape his work
differently. He might have been able to free himself even earlier from the
vessel of the Theosophical Society that had been necessary at that time for
the realization of his impulse.

> ... a way of working is to be endowed ... The nature of the
> Endowment lets us recognize that this way of working has its direct
> point of origin in that individuality whom we in the West have
> designated for aeons with the name Christian Rosenkreutz ... this way
> of working will enter the world as an endowment under the pro-
> tectorate of this individuality, Christian Rosenkreutz.[144]

In view of what has been said so far, we can perhaps better understand
how centrally involved the individuality of Christian Rosenkreutz was to
be in this attempt at an endowment—and in relation to Rudolf Steiner.
Rudolf Steiner separates himself from the aspect of the Endowment that
was to have 'an existence (substance) based in itself'; and yet he remains
within the Endowment as '... the interpreter of what is to be said in this
way about the matter's underlying intentions'.[145] Thus we understand
through his description that the Endowment with its way of working
stands under the protectorate of Christian Rosenkreutz, and that he,
Rudolf Steiner, is the interpreter of its spiritual intentions. We can turn to
a statement by Rudolf Steiner in order to grasp more fully the relationship
between two of the most important leaders of humanity. In the 5 October
1924 newsletter for members of the Anthroposophical Society, the supplement to the weekly *Das Goetheanum*, Rudolf Steiner reports about the
course he had just given for the priests of the Christian Community: 'Two
years later ... these priests felt the need to find a closer connection to the
Book of Revelation.—I believed I had something to contribute to finding
such a connection. My spiritual paths had made it possible for me to
follow the traces of the apocalyptist.'[146] Here Rudolf Steiner refers to
John the evangelist and apocalyptist whose essential being—according to
Rudolf Steiner's spiritual research—is identical with Christian Rosenkreutz. The spiritual connection between Rudolf Steiner and Christian
Rosenkreutz is self-evident in this statement.

The requirements for this special way of working appear to have been
partially fulfilled by the small circle that had received the 'sanction'—that
is, the calling—on 27 November 1911. The participant knows that both
the task and the way of working are 'purely spiritual'; he must also have

the 'will to place his own forces in service to what is positive about it'.[147]
Moreover, the participant must clearly and decisively acknowledge three
principles that can be understood as the foundation for this way of
working: '... the principle of the sovereignty of spiritual striving, the
principle of federalism, and the principle of the independence of all
spiritual striving as an absolute necessity for the spiritual future ...'[148]
Rudolf Steiner does not explicitly explain or clarify these three principles
in his address. Perhaps he could justifiably assume that those present
would already understand these central principles based on their years of
esoteric schooling under his guidance—which included the work with
the Mystery Dramas. Through his writings, his lectures, the esoteric
lessons and the ritual cultic work, he himself had given this group of
people many indications, exercises and personal instructions intended to
guide them in their spiritual striving to a sovereign, independent spiritual
situation. In this context, he had often told them that they should not
believe what he said but instead should create for themselves the thoughts
they had heard, i.e. they should test these thoughts for themselves as well!
In the lecture cycle *The Theosophy of the Rosicrucian*, held after the 1907
Congress in Munich, Rudolf Steiner spoke with great clarity about the
'Rosicrucian method': 'Anyone who cannot grasp Rosicrucian wisdom
with his thinking has not yet developed his logical understanding fully
enough.'[149] And likewise, the question in the title of the book *Wie erlangt
man Erkenntnisse der höheren Welten?* [How can one attain knowledge of
higher worlds?][150] is answered: through self-knowledge, i.e. through
'sovereignty of spiritual striving'.

By its very nature, the endowment of a Society for a Theosophical Art
and Way of Life was to contribute to the principle of federalism. The
word *federal* is derived from the Latin *fides* (faith), which also has in it the
sense of trust. Thus it is an affiliation of various members or participants
who are bound together through mutual trust. This trust serves as the basis
upon which the various entities, persons, etc., remain connected with one
another despite their independence.[151] The same is true in the Endowment: the tasks of the people described above are not given to the individual by appointment but rather by interpretation. Marie von Sivers,
later Marie Steiner-von Sivers, is 'interpreted from the Endowment itself'
as the curator of the Endowment,[152] while the other members of this
small circle are interpreted by Rudolf Steiner. She then takes up this task
of gathering other people for the Endowment, people who want to work
in this way. As a core quality of the Endowment, the principle of
federalism is related to the affiliation for which the conservator, Sophie
Stinde, will have oversight. But the way in which much of the

Endowment's work is to enter the world is intimately connected to its description—the principle of federalism is able to work out into the world. The modality or method would then be shaped so that independence in performing the designated task is maintained while the intention of this spiritual way of working is also preserved.

The third requirement follows from the first two—but it also represents the prerequisite for them. It concerns 'the independence of all spiritual striving as an absolute necessity for the spiritual future . . .'[153] In my view, the intent of these three aspects is significant: they are not intended to serve the individuals in the Endowment as achievements for the Endowment alone, or as elite ideals; instead they are to be carried out 'into humanity in the way [the circle] finds appropriate'.[154] It is at this point that the decision about what should be carried appropriately into humanity is granted to the small circle of people, a circle that is supposed to grow over time. Rudolf Steiner is not part of this circle but is the 'interpreter of . . . the matter's underlying intentions'.[155]

There are three further aspects that belong intimately to the Endowment's way of working; they are inwardly deeply rooted in the Rosicrucian stream. The first aspect concerns the starting point, i.e. how a person first enters this Endowment. It is based on a recognition of the person, but the recognition comes only when he or she fulfils a requirement: '. . . the will to become a member [of the Endowment] can originate only from the person who wants to become a member, no one else. And the fact that he is a member will become evident when the person is recognized as one. This relates only to the immediate future, only for the period preceding the next Three Kings Day, 6 January 1912.'[156] Rudolf Steiner does not indicate how it would continue from there. There are two dimensions here that must exist in a mutual relationship to one another: an independent, free will on the part of the person who wishes to become a member, and a recognition on the part of those responsible for the Endowment. Secondly, a law of existence is an integral part of this; it is given special emphasis here:

And one aspect of the eternal laws of existence is to take into consideration the principles of becoming as well . . . because everything is to be in a continuous state of becoming . . . What ought to happen is not based on words but on people—and not even on people but on what these people will *do*. It will exist in a living flow, a living development.[157]

Rudolf Steiner adds a basic principle to this: '*Recognition of the spiritual world as the fundamental reality*.'[158]

He compares the matter to a living tree because 'What this matter ought to become should never in any way be impaired by what it is.'[159] A sign of confidence in regard to the future of the attempt can be found in remarks Rudolf Steiner makes towards the end of the address. This can be heard both in his restrained but positive attitude and in his clear statement about the Theosophical Society:

> What you can take from everything that has been said here is that the matter will then continue. In its most profound principle, it will also differentiate itself from what the Theosophical Society is—because not one of the attributes expressed today can be applied to the Theosophical Society.[160]

Thus along with the aspect of free will in regard to the person who wishes to become a part, a member, of this way of working, and the recognition given to him, there is the aspect of becoming—but this is an aspect that must arise from continuity. More simply put, if nothing is there, nothing can become; without water, there is no river. Sometimes we can experience that arbitrariness wishes to negate continuity and through this negation becoming is misinterpreted. Only when the second aspect— becoming based on continuity—is present can a third aspect also arise: metamorphosis into something new. In summary, we see:

1. the starting point in free will and recognition;
2. the sustained becoming based on continuity;
3. a metamorphosis into something new arising out of becoming.

Here we see the expression of the Trinitarian principle that constitutes a fundamental element in Rosicrucianism. It can find expression in various forms and nuances but as a whole it is always and undeviatingly a matter of the Father principle (starting point), the Son principle (becoming-dying-change), and the Spirit principle (metamorphosis-resurrection). Thus it does not seem strange that this Trinitarian element should appear exactly where an endowment impulse is to take place under the protectorate of Christian Rosenkreutz.

Most of the people who had been present at this address had seen the second Mystery Drama, *The Soul's Probation*, a few months before, in August 1911. They had heard the words of Celia in the ninth scene as she spoke with Thomas:

> Out of the Godhead rose the human soul;
> dying, it can descend to depths of being;
> it will, in time, release from death the spirit.[161]

The end of the address contains a subtle expression of confidence in the future of this attempt.[162] Rudolf Steiner comments again about the founding of the Theosophical Society and its continued existence. There is a rather serious implication in his statement concerning the effect of Ahriman. He says: '... an ideal spiritual counterweight to everything connected with founding something in the outer world must be created...' Then something pivotal follows:

> ... that this branch of our Endowment, the branch for theosophical art, is to accomplish something that provides a counterweight to things connected to the ahrimanic on the physical plane ... In all respects, spiritual life must be completely evident as the basis for what we do. In all respects, the point is that what is spiritual forms the ground on which we stand. This was attempted during the drama festivals in Munich, and in the construction of the lodge building in Stuttgart—at least to the extent it was possible under the existing circumstances; but it was attempted everywhere in such a way that the spiritual moment was the decisive factor. This is the *conditio sine qua non*, the requisite condition without which nothing is to happen.[163]

The 'spiritual moment' should, in fact, have occurred on 27 November and 15 December 1911, but because of one person, because of Alice Sprengel, this 'spiritual moment' could not be realized in the context of the Endowment.

It may seem odd to us that an endowment that stood under the protectorate of Christian Rosenkreutz, for which Rudolf Steiner served as the interpreter of its spiritual principles from the spiritual world, and which was to be heard at that time as a 'second call' from the spiritual world, nevertheless could not come into being because of the participation of this one person. But, as we can come to realize, spiritual laws work differently than physical laws. In her 1947 mimeographed publication Marie Steiner wrote: 'After the year had ended and when the next Three Kings Day had passed with no further nominations forthcoming, a person in the audience posed a question to Rudolf Steiner about when this might happen. His response was that it had not happened—and that this, too, was an answer.'[164]

9 'It Was an Attempt'

In her epilogue to the 1947 mimeographed edition, Marie Steiner quotes from a lecture given by Rudolf Steiner on 21 August 1915 and published for the first time in 1989, five years after the 1984 publication of the Endowment address in Rudolf Steiner's collected works.[165] In this lecture Rudolf Steiner recalls the situation in regard to the attempt at an endowment and describes it:

> Because certain impossible symptoms had manifested in our Society, it was announced one autumn that it had become necessary to found a certain more internal society in which I first attempted to allocate certain titles to a number of close colleagues and long-standing Society members. I had assumed that they would work independently in the sense of these titles. At that time I said: If something is to happen, the members will hear about it by Three Kings Day. No one heard anything so it follows that a Society for a Theosophical Art and Way of Life does not exist at all. That is actually self-evident since a report of it was not made to anyone—just as it is self-evident that a report would have been distributed if the matter had been implemented. The way in which the matter was understood in one particular case made it impossible. It was an attempt.[166]

This address of 21 August 1915 was given during a very turbulent period because the situation—already difficult in 1911—had grown increasingly serious. Alice Sprengel and her friends Dr Heinrich Goesch and his wife Gertrud had a role in this. It is unnecessary to give a full account of these events that affected the Anthroposophical Society founded by members on 28 December 1912, in Cologne. However, Hella Wiesberger's summary, augmented by several relevant aspects, can offer some insight into them. Hella Wiesberger writes:

> Rudolf Steiner's marriage to Marie von Sivers at Christmas 1914 had ... engendered odd mystical eccentricities in one member in particular, Alice Sprengel. These were taken up and used by Heinrich and Gertrud Goesch to attack Rudolf Steiner personally. Since they did so openly within the Society, Rudolf Steiner requested that the matter also be cleared up through the Society. There followed weeks of discussion that ended in the exclusion of the three. Rudolf Steiner and

Marie Steiner had participated neither in the discussions nor in the decision to exclude.[167]

Hella Wiesberger describes how Alice Sprengel reacted to the fact that she played the role of Theodora in the Mystery Dramas (1910–13), and also how she regarded Rudolf Steiner's 'interpretation' of her as keeper of the seal in the 1911 Endowment attempt. Alice Sprengel believed she had undergone great and significant incarnations. A letter from an English-woman, Mary Peet, offers us a glimpse into this strange situation. Mary Peet had been connected with Rudolf Steiner's work since 1910 but had begun as a pupil of Annie Besant. She had moved to Dornach with other members in 1914 and worked actively for the anthroposophical movement. Her letter is addressed to Alice Sprengel. A few excerpts provide insight into Alice Sprengel's psychological condition:

> Dear Fräulein Sprengel! I did not want to wait any longer to express to you my indignation over your shameful behaviour in regard to Dr Steiner and Frau Dr Steiner ... If someone [Alice Sprengel] considers herself to be the reincarnation of David and the Virgin Mary there is not much more to be said; anyone who indulges in such notions places himself beyond the realm of logic and reason.[168]

Whenever Rudolf Steiner refers to Alice Sprengel, he almost always calls her the keeper of the seal. Dr Heinrich Goesch wrote to Rudolf Steiner in August 1915: 'I have this knowledge that I acquired under the guidance of the keeper of the seal for the Society for a Theosophical Art and Way of Life; its protector is Christian Rosenkreutz ...'[169] Rudolf Steiner read this letter aloud to the members with the comment: 'The so-called keeper of the seal is, I think, known to all of you, and I would only add that this keeper of the seal sent a number of letters during the last few months—some to me, some to Frau Dr Steiner.'[170] Referring then to the approach of Sigmund Freud, Rudolf Steiner provides the members with a detailed description of the complexities in the Goesch-Sprengel relationship, a description that illustrates how thoroughly Rudolf Steiner had grappled with Freud. '... According to Freudian theory, everything that lived in the soul of the friend, the "keeper of the seal" came to the surface.'[171]

Before we put this unfortunate theme behind us we need to call to mind three esoterically relevant dimensions. First, we cannot really assess what it meant at that time and for the further development of anthroposophy that the Endowment was obstructed by one person's pathological state. Second, Alice Sprengel had told Dr Goesch in detail about the Endowment. Even if he had been present on 15 December 1911, it had been her task as keeper of the seal to have kept the inner secret—but she did not remain silent. Third, it is noteworthy that Rudolf Steiner so often uses the expression 'keeper of the seal' (*Siegelbewahrer*, the German word's masculine form) in his statements. But in this case he uses the *Siegelbewahrerin* (the feminine form) instead. This form of the word points directly to the fact that anything that might remain of this task's esoteric content had been cast aside as a direct result of these events.

In this connection, it should be mentioned that one year later Marie Steiner provided financial support for Alice Sprengel, who found herself in urgent financial need. By then, Alice Sprengel—along with Dr Heinrich Goesch and Gertrud Goesch—had been excluded from the Society by its Central Executive Council, and she had also moved away from Dornach. Since—understandably—few were inclined to help her, Marie Steiner wrote a letter to a member, Fräulein Wernicke, who was still in contact with Alice Sprengel:

> ... based on a general human compassion for the urgent situation described, there is no recourse for me other than to assume that debt and to cover it. Of course, I must also ask you not to mention my name in connection with this. First, it would not be pleasant for Fräulein Sprengel herself; and, second, I would not want to acquire the reputation of someone who wishes somehow to accommodate Fräulein Sprengel.[172]

10 THE CONTINUING EFFECT OF THE ENDOWMENT IMPULSE

We have seen how the impulse for an endowment of this special way of working among a group of people represents a significant social impulse related to the individuality of Christian Rosenkreutz. We can broaden our view from a present-day perspective when we recognize that this impulse appears from time to time, mostly after longer intervals. In this context, for instance, Rudolf Steiner refers to the early seventeenth-century writings of Johann Valentin Andreae. The best known of these is *The Chymical Wedding of Christian Rosenkreutz anno 1459* (written in 1603, published in 1616); he also wrote the *Fama Fraternitatis* (1614) and the *Confessio Fraternitatis* (1615). In speaking about the *Confessio*, Rudolf Steiner notes:

> It was an address to the heads of state, the statesmen of his time; it was an *attempt* [emphasis VS] to found a social order intended to correspond to the true reality of something rather than to its maya . . . The Thirty Years War began in 1618.—The conditions it engendered swept away the most noble elements sought by the *Fama Fraternitatis* and the *Confessio.*[173]

This seventeenth-century attempt found expression in the books of Johann Valentin Andreae who, according to Rudolf Steiner, was inspired through a lofty Rosicrucian initiation.[174] We might expect such a social impulse to be undermined—even attacked—by counterforces. The same thing happened with the French Revolution that began in 1789. The full intention of its Trinitarian impulse—*Liberté, Fraternité, Égalité*—could not be realized either.

In regard to the attempt to endow a society for a theosophical art and way of life, it neither can nor will be asserted here that the attempt was in vain or that it failed completely. Thirty-six years later—in 1947—Marie Steiner could take a positive tone in her prologue to the address. Today her words sound poetic and future-oriented, and they may occupy a significant place in our considerations:

> . . . his [Rudolf Steiner's] form of expression varies depending on the task being described . . . it can allow an intimation of a light to manifest through the language, a light that necessarily remains partially concealed because words are inadequate. Something like a gentle veil

covers it, but through this veil the impulses pointing to the future can be active. Time and again, he placed into our souls those forces that direct us towards later activity, seeds of the future that might come to life and unfold after having undergone a soul-sleep ... The passage through death and immersion in chaos ... offer assurance of a later revival of the spiritual impulse as it undergoes metamorphoses to achieve higher levels of existence. The law of transformation into new forms of existence prevails in the microcosm as in the macrocosm, in earthly life as in planetary life.[175]

Of all the people around Rudolf Steiner, Marie Steiner was the one most able to understand continuity, in both its inner and outer aspects. She was able to maintain and cultivate seeds of the future in her soul during the 23 years of her life following Rudolf Steiner's death—seeds that had been given by Rudolf Steiner himself. Although she often expressed her disappointment in the inadequacy of people for whom the tasks had proven to be too mighty, she never became nihilistic, never gave up hope. Her private publication of the Endowment document—to which this reflection is dedicated—serves as an important demonstration of this. Her physical and spiritual eyes were schooled in perceiving the human situation as well as the inner schooling needed by each individual; she could read whether an individual had the capacity to withstand the great ordeals of the age. As Rudolf Steiner's first esoteric pupil and his close colleague throughout those many years, it had been possible for Marie Steiner to experience various people during their ordeals and to support them when it was appropriate to do so. Thus, from the beginning, the task of the Endowment came to her:

> ... Fräulein von Sivers will be recognized as curator by the Endowment itself [Christian Rosenkreutz] ... Fräulein von Sivers is interpreted as the curator of the Endowment. And her task in the immediate future will be to do what can be done in the sense of this Endowment in order to solicit (gather) a circle of members appropriate for it ...[176]

The Endowment and its original interpretations remained an attempt, but seven of the eight people who had been called to certain tasks—Alice Sprengel was the tragic exception—accomplished great things during their lifetimes as provided by their karma; these tasks unite their identity inseparably with the development of anthroposophy and with the individuality of Rudolf Steiner in the twentieth century. We can imagine or even sense that these seven people, like the others who had been present at the original ritual gathering on 27 November 1911, continued to work under the protectorate of Christian Rosenkreutz even if it was not in the sense that might have been made possible had the Endowment entered into existence. These people are united by a shared karma through the fact that they had been interpreted for their individual tasks at that time.

My thanks again go to Uwe Werner, the archivist at the Goetheanum, for allowing me to make use of unpublished documents.[177] In these documents we discover that the first and only direct result of the Endowment was the publication of the 1912/1913 *Calendar of the Soul*— although it was not mentioned in the meeting on 15 December 1911. It appears that the decision to publish this calendar was made at that time, and Imme von Eckardtstein made the drawings for it.

It must be presumed that Imme von Eckardtstein was also present during Marie Steiner's illness and her sojourn in Portorose, and that the drawings for the *Calendar* were made there. We may also assume that Rudolf Steiner was inwardly engaged with the contents of the *Soul Calendar* verses despite the turbulence of 1911 and his many other obligations during that year.

Since Rudolf Steiner's *Soul Calendar* first appeared at Easter 1912, people around the world have been living with its verses. In them, Rudolf Steiner steps forward as the great interpreter of nature, the soul, the cosmos. In his foreword to the first edition, Rudolf Steiner 'endows' a

Wichtige Neu-Erscheinung.

Zu Ostern 1912 erscheint im philosophisch-theosophischen Verlage (Berlin W, Motzstraße 17) ein

THEOSOPHISCHER KALENDER.

Derselbe wird enthalten die für Theosophen wichtigen Kalenderdaten von Ostern 1912 bis Ostern 1913; außerdem die Angaben über die Tages-, Sonnen- und Mondenconstellationen durch

intuitive Bilder und Symbole,

die von einem unserer Mitglieder herrühren, sowie einen

Seelen-Kalender mit Meditationen für jede Woche des Jahres.

Announcement for the 1912 Calendar of the Soul

most significant indication, namely how the individual human being can develop his own capacities to become an interpreter.[178] He does not offer 'prescriptions' in the manner of a theosophical pedant; instead, we are shown the way to the living weaving of the soul as it can come to be in the future. Everything pertaining to souls takes on an individual coloration. For this very reason, however, each *soul* will find its way in accord with its own particular coloration. It would be easy to say: The soul should meditate as described here if it wants to cultivate a measure of self-knowledge. A statement of this kind is *not* made—human beings should find their own stimulus and direction on a 'path of knowledge'; the 'path of knowledge' is not to be followed pedantically.

In his foreword to the second printing in 1918, Rudolf Steiner gives an even more precise orientation for the person wishing to undertake these exercises.

> For each week, a verse is given in this calendar that allows the soul to experience what is happening during this week as part of the life of the whole of the year. What this life lets sound in the soul when the soul unites with it will be expressed in the verse. The intention is a healthy 'feeling of being at one' with the course of nature and an associated powerful 'finding of oneself' that arises from it. The thought is that empathy with the course of the world in the sense of these verses is something the soul longs for—if only it understands itself rightly.[179]

In the Endowment address, Rudolf Steiner says in reference to the 'theosophical way of life': 'What will be encompassed by "theosophical way of life" is still in a completely germinal state; the preparations for this first have to be made. These preparations can then lead to an understanding of what it intends.'[180] When we look at Rudolf Steiner's work in the years following the end of the First World War in 1918, we recognize that Rudolf Steiner—as the great initiate of the twentieth century—endowed impulses for humanity in every area of life, in education, medicine, agriculture, eurythmy (which was born in Berlin in December 1911 and January 1912) and social life, not to mention art and other areas. He did not just endow them for decades but for centuries. Even though the Endowment of 15 December 1911 did not achieve fulfilment, seeds were planted for the future, especially through the *Calendar of the Soul*, which can call forth metamorphoses in every human soul when cultivated in daily practice.

APPENDIX

AN ESOTERIC-SOCIAL IMPULSE FOR THE FUTURE

THE ATTEMPT AT AN 'ENDOWMENT' OF A SOCIETY FOR A THEOSOPHICAL ART AND WAY OF LIFE

Address, Berlin, 15 December 1911 (Morning)[181]

An Impulse for the Future Given through Rudolf Steiner and what Became of it
Foreword by Marie Steiner[182]

In view of the difficulties of our age and what little of life remains viable, it seems an urgent duty to rescue what we still can of Rudolf Steiner's impulses and words.[183] He discussed much of this in earnest conversations only within intimates circles—at certain turning points in events that affected the further tasks and goals of the movement he inaugurated; notes exist, but they are neither abundant nor exhaustive. Even when there are gaps in these notes or perhaps when they fail to pick up the finer nuances, it is still possible to get a good sense for how his form of expression varies depending on the task being described. This form can be sculpturally contoured and solid; or—dissolving away—it can allow an intimation of a light to manifest through the language, a light that necessarily remains partially concealed because words are inadequate. Something like a gentle veil covers it, but through this veil the impulses pointing to the future can be active. Time and again, he placed into our souls those forces that direct us towards later activity, seeds of the future that might come to life and unfold after having undergone a soul-sleep. These seeds were all too often buried beneath the hubbub of everyday life or caught up in the maelstrom of events and swept away. Among the souls granted such seeds of the future there were certainly many in whom these seeds could give rise to new life and striving. But there were also some who were unable to offer nourishment to these seeds—as in the Gospel's image of the stony field. The organic lawfulness of nature applies not only to nature itself, but to souls as well. Some of what falls spiritually into our souls either hardens or withers; other things prove to be viable seeds and transform themselves into new forms of existence. The passage through death and immersion in chaos with its confusing forces of upheaval offer assurance of a later revival of the spiritual impulse as it undergoes metamorphoses to achieve higher levels of existence. The law of transformation into new forms of existence prevails in the microcosm as in the macrocosm, in earthly life as in planetary life. Again and again, religions ascended to new heights of knowledge as they travelled this path; they demonstrated it and explained it in images appropriate to each folk group and nation—cosmically and in accord with the course of time, they cast a light into the hidden depths.

When this development had reached a certain culmination and a danger of philosophical abstraction had emerged, the old images and signs were no longer adequate for capturing the newly pulsating life. The Christian impulse entered here, bringing with it the great turning point. However, as this impulse emerged from the darkness of the catacombs into the outer world, the danger also arose that it would be rigidified in dogma. Thus its burgeoning forces of life sought out new avenues— avenues within secret societies that refused to bow to the authority of the princes of the Church and the edicts of Church councils; as a result, these societies were persecuted as heretical. The substance of these societies was hidden from the outer world and lived once again in signs and symbols. They gave a new impetus to art, an impetus that made its first appearance in works of Gothic architecture where the organic growth of plants was integrated into stone. This new life flowed even into names—names that contained what the soul needed to acquire as guiding forces if it was to develop in a healthy way before it achieved autonomy. However humanity's education towards autonomy—an autonomy into which the newly awakened ego power was to pour itself—first needed to pass through abstract intellectualism. This abstract intellectualism separated souls from their primal spiritual origin for a period of time; once the soul had endured the frigid iciness of isolation and taken hold of the higher ego, it could find itself again in the spirit. Knowledge of nature detached from the spirit no longer gives the soul the forces it needs to stand upright. Spirits had to demolish worlds in order for this to be experienced and recognized. We are now standing in the midst of shattered worlds—and a new quest for a solution to the riddles of destiny has begun. Rudolf Steiner's life's work can offer a response to this seeking and questioning. He had a command of all that modern exact science encompasses; and he is able to reveal for us the spirit and its impelling force that lies concealed behind this science—a spirit once hidden in the old names. Through him we are able to sense the forces that give impulse, those forces at work behind the names. We were thus given life rafts for the inevitable ship- wreck to come, but we were not yet mature enough to grasp or make use of them. Souls were not sufficiently awake; they were still caught up in the old views. Attempts made in a social context met the strongest possible opposition from the outside world. An overwhelming pain can take hold of us when we see how little prepared we were to make fruitful what had been offered; how little we were able to be suitable instruments for the fiery spirit of the helper sent in time of need. Standing on the ruins of shattered worlds, we must now turn to the fragmentary notes that remain in order to bring to consciousness the word that was preserved but not grasped with sufficient fire; and we must elevate it to the level of ego humanity through our own individual work. Rudolf Steiner attempted to lead us to individual freedom not only along the paths of philosophy and science but also through an education within esoteric life that would gradually transform the old relationship of dependence on a teacher into the impulse of freedom and responsibility for the spirit. Souls who experience themselves as rooted in the spirit must be tested. When such a trial is sought out by the individual, it always calls forth an accelerated karma; it must also bring to light what otherwise would prefer to remain hidden. Attempts drawn from deep cosmic foundations by spiritual forces with the goal of elevating humanity's development to a higher level have often failed as a result of such trials. This was the case with the French Revolution as well as in the time before the World Wars of this (the twentieth) century.

Rudolf Steiner first spoke about such future-oriented tasks to a very small circle of his pupils; he tried to guide souls towards the meaning of those far-distant tasks that must arise from human will freed of selfish egoism. He repeated these words before a larger circle convened by him at the General Meeting [of the Theosophical Society] on 15 December 1911. This gathering was not part of the proceedings of the General Meeting itself; he made clear that it lay outside of the Society's programme. He began his address in a particularly solemn and impressive manner. This may explain why the first part of the address is only briefly noted and his words are not recounted in their entirety. He emphasized that the content of this lecture would stand completely apart from everything he had offered until then. It concerned a direct communication from the spiritual world. It was like a call proffered to humanity—to be followed by a period of waiting for any echo that might arise in response. He said that—as a rule—such a call would only occur three times. If the call falls on deaf ears the first and second times, then sounds for a third time and again goes unheeded, it is taken back into the spiritual world for a long period of time. This call had already been brought to humanity once before:

unfortunately it found no echo.[184] This would be the second time. This is a purely spiritual matter. The relationships and stipulations become more difficult with each futile attempt.

Continuing then with the significant points we find preserved in the notes, Rudolf Steiner said:

My dear friends! At this moment, it is incumbent on me to bring into this wider circle an intention already known within a more intimate circle.[185] It must be emphasized, however, that what will be said now has absolutely no connection to what has happened earlier in this General Meeting; nor is it related in any way to earlier proceedings. This does not preclude consideration of these matters during later proceedings should there be a wish to do so.

If we survey what is happening in the world today we will have to say to ourselves: The modern world is actually full of ideals. And if we ask ourselves: Are these ideals represented straightforwardly and honestly by those who believe in them and put themselves in service to them?—we will, in many instances, have to answer: Yes, that is true. It is so to the extent that individual people can bring faith and devotion to the matter. —We might ask: How much is usually required when someone—an individual or a society—calls such a representation of ideals into life? We would then have to answer, based on our observation of life itself: In most cases, we could say that everything is required. Above all, what is required is an absolute and unqualified acknowledgement of the ideal that has been adopted. The basis for putting forth such an ideal is nearly always a requirement of absolute and utter agreement with the ideal itself. And non-compliance with such an agreement usually evokes some kind of negative criticism of the person who does not agree.

These words are meant to characterize how the underlying principle for bringing people together arose quite naturally in the course of humanity's evolution; this is not the time to give voice to doubts about the validity of such a principle. But now a possibility will be presented (made available) to you in order to add something to what all the world has striven for in bringing people together—in societies, associations, and so on. It is actually impossible to express this element in words since what can be said can never serve as a true measure for the validity of such a thing. It is in the nature of what a human being is able to think that he may fall into contradiction with reality in the moment he tries to express what he has thought; he is forced into this contradiction by the very act of expressing the thought. Much must be said at this juncture that is not in agreement with what is often asserted in the world as true. Thus it must be said: It is possible that an assertion of belief in something may no longer be valid when this assertion of belief is given expression. I would like to offer a simple example to demonstrate the potential danger of becoming untruthful by merely expressing something. And I would like to have this simple, basic example I am offering understood in the sense of Rosicrucian principles that have existed since the thirteenth century.

Let us assume someone expresses his situation in the immediate present by stating, 'I am silent.' This is categorically untrue; what he expressed has no truth in it. Thus I ask you, dear friends, to recognize the possibility that a verbal expression of belief in something may be inherently self-contradictory. You can conclude that what is expressed in the simple example 'I am silent' applies to a myriad of situations in the world, and these situations occur time and time again.

What results from such a fact? One result is that people find themselves in an especially difficult position when they try to affiliate in some way with one another in order to represent something; they are unable to affiliate with one another in regard to what they cherish most unless their affiliation is based in the supersensible world and not in the sensory world. And if we understand what we have been able to accrue over time from all that more recent occultism has given us, we will realize that representing certain aspects of this occultism, bringing them to the attention of the world, is an absolute necessity for the immediate future (time). Therefore, in contrast to all of the principles of societies, in contrast to all the organizations that have been possible until recently, an attempt must now be made to create something completely new, something born entirely out of the spirit of that occultism we speak of so often in our circles. But this can be done only by focusing our gaze on something positive, on something that already exists in the world as a reality—on something that can be cultivated, as such. Realities in our sense of the word, however, are only those things that belong first and foremost to the supersensible world because the whole sensory world appears to us as a replica of the supersensible world. Thus an attempt will be made, the kind of attempt that must be made out of the supersensible world—an attempt made not to found, but to endow an association of people.

Under other circumstances I once highlighted the difference between *founding* and *endowing*. But that was many years ago.[186] It was not understood at the time and practically no one has given any thought to this difference since then. Thus those spiritual powers that are placed before you under the *symbolum* of the Rose Cross looked away from the attempts to carry this difference out into the world.

This attempt must be made anew—and in an energetic way this time—
to discover whether an association that is not founded but rather endowed
can be successful. If success is not achieved, it will have failed again for a
while (and thus must be deferred again for a while).

Therefore this is the time to announce to you that a way of working is
to be endowed among those who will find themselves appropriately a part
of it. The nature of the Endowment lets us recognize that this way of
working has its direct point of origin in that individuality whom we in the
West have designated for aeons with the name Christian Rosenkreutz.
What can be said today about this Endowment remains preliminary; what
could be endowed up to now relates only to a part of this Endowment, an
endowment that is to enter the world fully as possibilities for it arise. What
could be endowed earlier corresponds to one department, to one branch
of this Endowment—namely the artistic representation of Rosicrucian
occultism.

The first point I have to communicate to you is this: what will enter
into life will be a way of working under the immediate protectorate of the
individuality whom we designate with the name he has had in the outside
world for two incarnations—this way of working will enter the world as
an endowment under the protectorate of this individuality, Christian
Rosenkreutz. It can be characterized—for the time being, for the
immediate future—by the provisional name *Society for a Theosophical Art
and Way of Life*. This is not its definitive name; instead, a definitive name
will emerge when initial preparations for carrying this Endowment out
into the world have been completed. What will be encompassed by
'theosophical way of life' is still in a completely germinal state; the
preparations for this first have to be made. These preparations can then
lead to an understanding of what it intends. However, in many ways what
can be understood under the concept of theosophical art has already had
its genesis in our efforts during the performances in Munich. It had a
particularly significant start through the efforts to create our centre in
Stuttgart. And the founding of the *Johannes-Bauverein* [The Johannes
Building Association] was another significant beginning for our understanding of such a matter. These have all had their beginning. There is
something identifiable connected with them that can be sanctioned to a
certain extent as tried and tested.

The point is that a purely spiritual task should awaken within the
working circle, a task that will find its fulfilment in a spiritual way of
working and in what results from such a way of working. Furthermore,
no one will be able to become a member of this working circle (this way
of working) for any reason other than some (sort of) will to place his own

forces in service to what is positive about it. You might say I am using many words and phrases that are perhaps not entirely understandable. This must be the case in matters like the one being considered here because the matter itself must be taken hold of directly from within its life.

Within this Endowment it has already been possible to start by creating a very small circle, one might even say a tiny circle, based on purely occult principles (laws); this circle is to see its responsibility in collaborative work on the task at hand. Initially, the way this very tiny circle is formed makes possible a beginning for this Endowment so that what our spiritual stream is might be separated from me [Rudolf Steiner] in a certain sense, and the Endowment provided with an existence (substance) based in itself—an existence founded in itself!

Thus, to begin with, this small circle appears before you with *this* sanction: as such, it has received its task by virtue of its own acknowledgement of our spiritual stream; in a certain way, it sees the principle of the sovereignty of spiritual striving, the principle of federalism, and independence of all spiritual striving as an absolute necessity for the spiritual future—and it is to carry this into humanity in the way it finds appropriate. Thus within the endowment under consideration I myself will serve solely as the interpreter of the principles which, as such, are only present in the spiritual world—the interpreter of what is to be said in this way about the matter's underlying intentions.

On the other hand, a curator will first be appointed for the external nurturing of this Endowment. And since there is nothing but duty connected with the offices created—no honours, no high rank—it will be impossible from the very beginning for any rivalries or other misunderstandings to arise if the matter is rightly understood. Thus Fräulein von Sivers will be recognized as curator by the Endowment itself. This recognition is nothing other than a recognition interpreted from the Endowment itself; there are no appointments, only interpretations. Fräulein von Sivers is interpreted as the curator of the Endowment. And her task in the immediate future will be to do what can be done in the sense of this Endowment in order to solicit (gather) a circle of members appropriate for it—not in an external sense but so that the Endowment will allow individuals to approach it who possess the earnest will to collaborate in this way of working.

In the broader sense, within this one branch of our Endowment a number of ancillary branches will be created. Once again, several individuals who have been tested within our spiritual movement will take their places as leading personalities in these ancillary branches—in so far as these already exist—and they will have the corresponding duties. At the outset, this too is an interpretation, and in this way the office of leading such an individual ancillary branch is delegated to a particular person. An archdeacon will be interpreted for each of these ancillary branches. We will have an ancillary branch for art in general. It was published [trans. made known] in the small circle that Fräulein Eckardtstein will be the archdeacon for art in general. This was done in express recognition of what this personality has accomplished on behalf of theosophical art in general over the course of the last years: Fräulein Eckardtstein. In addition, it was published that the curator Fräulein von Sivers will be the provisional archdeacon for literature. Further, it was published that the archdeacon for the art of architecture shall be our friend Dr Felix Peipers; for the art of music, our friend Mr Adolph Arenson; for painting, our friend Mr Hermann Linde.

The work to be done here is essentially inner work; and what will initially appear before the world is work carried in absolute freedom by these individual personalities. In a certain sense, it will be necessary for a collegial collaboration to be accomplished among those who belong to this way of working; this collaboration will have to occur in a completely different way than has been the case up to now in other (customary) organizations. And we will need (have to have) someone whose task it is to watch over this activity. The role of conservator is being created to watch over this collegial collaboration; this office will be given to Fräulein Sophie Stinde. Related to the collegial affiliation itself is the way the affiliation is achieved. All this will require more work in the near future; it must still be accomplished. If the way of collaboration—in other words, the principle of organization—is to be achieved, is to appear in the world, we will need a seal conservator. Fräulein Sprengel was published as the conservator of the seal, while Dr Carl Unger will be the secretary.

Initially, it will be a matter of this small, tiny circle. Do not regard it as something that seeks to appear immodestly in the world saying, 'Here I am.' Regard it instead as something that seeks to be nothing more than a seed around which the matter can organize itself. It will be organized so that—by the upcoming Three Kings Day—a number of members of this association will be interpreted. This means that by then a number of members will have received a communication asking them to consider whether they want to affiliate themselves. This is done to ensure from the outset the greatest degree of freedom in this connection (along these lines) because the will to become a member can originate only from the person who wants to become a member. And the fact that he is a member will become evident when the person is recognized as one. This relates only to the immediate future, only for the period preceding the next Three Kings Day, 6 January 1912.

Thus in what is now before us we have a matter that by its very nature reveals itself as an element flowing out of the spiritual world. It will continue to demonstrate that it is flowing out of the spiritual world through the fact that membership will always be based solely on the representation and recognition of spiritual interests and the exclusion of everything—*everything*—personal.

The act of making this announcement—the very fact of this announcement itself—is a deviation from older occult principles. Thus the claim will not be made here that might be put forth by a person who says, in reference to the present (to the present moment): I am silent. This matter is, in fact, being announced; and this act should take place in the full consciousness that it is being announced. But, of course, as soon as someone demonstrates he has virtually no understanding of today's announcement, he cannot in any way be advised to belong to such a way of working.—I am not referring to this as a society or anything like one.—Because becoming a member of such a circle, such a way of working can only result from an absolutely free will. You will see, however, that if something like this is to take place—if the singular character of our time allows something like this to happen—it will then really be possible to work in the sense of acknowledging the spiritual principle, the principle that the spiritual, supersensible world forms the basis not only of all nature and all history but also of all human activity that appears in the world. And you will see that it will be impossible for any respectable person to belong to such an association if he is not in agreement with it. If you think that what is being said here is quite peculiar then I would ask you to take it in this way: It has occurred in full consciousness that all aspects of the laws, the eternal laws of existence are observed in the process.

My dear friends, it would be possible at this point to sin against the spirit of what should happen here were someone to go out into the world now and say: This or that was founded here. Not only was absolutely nothing founded, but the fact of the matter is that it will be impossible at any given time to give a definition of what is to happen because everything is to be in a continuous state of becoming [development]. What should actually take place through what was said today cannot yet be described. There are no definitions for it, no descriptions can be given, and everything that might be said would become untrue in the moment it was uttered. What ought to happen is not based on words but on people—and not even on people but on what these people will *do*. It will exist in a living flow, a living development. Thus today no other principle will be set forth than the one (the first) principle: *Recognition of the spiritual world as the fundamental reality.*

All additional principles will be created in the course of the matter's development alone. Just as a tree is not the same now as it was a moment ago but has something new added to it, so will this matter be like a living tree. What this matter ought to become should never be in any way impaired by what it is. Thus if someone were to try to define what has been identified here as a beginning, as some kind of founding, as this or that thing in the outer world, he would immediately succumb to the same untruth found in the expression 'I am silent' when it is applied to what he is actually doing. In any event, the person who in some way or another uses these or similar words to characterize the matter expresses something incorrect. Thus to begin with—since everything will be in a state of becoming—the point is simply that those personalities come together who want something like this. The matter depends solely upon indivi-duals coming together who want something like this. Then it will con-tinue! What you can take from everything that has been said here is that the matter will then continue. In its most profound principle, it will also differentiate itself from what the Theosophical Society is—because not one of the attributes expressed today can be applied to the Theosophical Society.

I had to speak about this matter for the simple reason that things organically (organizationally) connected to this Endowment have already become public knowledge in our Theosophical Society. And because through this Endowment, through the creation of this Endowment—in the sense of intentions that are, in truth, not to be found in the physical world and, in truth, have nothing to do with Ahriman—an ideal spiritual counterweight (counter-image) to everything connected with founding something in the outer world must be created. Thus only in this sense can a relation, a correspondence (a connection) be seen to what already exists, i.e. that this branch of our Endowment, the branch for theosophical art, is to accomplish something that provides a counterweight to things con-nected to the ahrimanic on the physical plane.

The hope is that the presence of this branch of our Endowment will create a splendid example (model), and that the other branch will likewise be of service because what should appear as art in the theosophical movement—if we use this expression today—must, in fact, be something that flows into our culture from spiritual worlds. In all respects, spiritual life must be completely evident as the basis for what we do. It will be impossible to confuse or to mistake this ideal-spiritual movement for some other movement that comes from the outer world and attempts to designate itself, for example, as also part of the 'theosophical movement'. In all respects, the point is that what is spiritual forms the ground on which we stand. This was attempted during the drama festivals in Munich, in the construction of the lodge building in Stuttgart—at least to the extent it was possible under the existing circumstances; but everywhere it was attempted in such a way that the spiritual moment was the decisive factor. This is the *conditio sine qua non*, the requisite condition without which nothing is to happen. [A lacuna in the notes.]

Those who have already penetrated a little into the matter at hand will understand me in this regard. These words are said less for the content than for the guidelines they provide.

From the epilogue by Marie Steiner in the edition published by her

After the year had ended and when the next Three Kings Day had passed with no further nominations forthcoming, a person in the audience posed a question to Rudolf Steiner about when this might happen. His response was that it had not happened—and that this, too, was an answer.

Several years later, on 21 August 1915, he returned to the matter during a lecture in Dornach. At that time he said the following:

Because certain impossible symptoms had manifested in our Society, it was announced one autumn that it had become necessary to found a certain more internal society in which I first attempted to assign certain titles to a number of close colleagues and long-standing Society members. I had assumed that they would work independently in the sense of these titles. At that time I said: If something is to happen, the members will hear about it by Three Kings Day. No one heard anything so it follows that a Society for a Theosophical Art and Way of Life does not exist at all. That is actually self-evident since a report of it was not made to anyone—just as it is self-evident that a report would have been distributed if the matter had been implemented. The way in which the matter was understood in a particular case made it impossible. It was an attempt.

NOTES

The references to Rudolf Steiner's works below are to the original German editions with a literal English translation of the title in brackets. The passages quoted in the text have been translated directly from the German unless otherwise noted. The 'GA' numbers refer to the catalogue number of the *Gesamtausgabe* or collected works in the original German as published by the Rudolf Steiner Verlag, Switzerland. The dates of the cited lectures are also given to facilitate the identification of the lectures in the relevant English-language edition.

Citations are given in full the first time they appear in the text. Works cited only by title and GA number are by Rudolf Steiner.

1. See *Anthroposophie wird Kunst. Der Münchner Kongress 1907 und die Gegenwart* [Anthroposophy becomes art. The 1907 Munich Congress and the present time], ed. Karl Lierl and Florian Roder (Anthroposophische Gesellschaft in Deutschland, Arbeitszentrum, München 2008).
2. See *Die Theosophie des Rosenkreuzers* [The theosophy of the Rosicrucian] (GA 99).
3. Rudolf Steiner, *Four Mystery Plays*, trans. Ruth and Hans Pusch (SteinerBooks/Anthroposophic Press, 2007). The Goetheanum in Switzerland offers performances of Rudolf Steiner's Mystery Dramas at regular intervals.
4. Lecture of 12 January 1910 (given for members in Stockholm). There is no stenographic record. On this theme see the notes to Rudolf Steiner, *Das Ereignis der Christus-Erscheinung in der ätherischen Welt* [The event of Christ's appearance in the etheric world] (GA 118), p. 229.
5. See *Okkulte Geschichte, Esoterische Betrachtungen karmischer Zusammenhänge von Persönlichkeiten und Ereignissen der Weltgeschichte* [Occult history, esoteric observations on karmic connections between personalities and events in world history] (GA 126).
6. Ibid. p. 113.
7. 'Die Grundsteinlegung des Stuttgarter Hauses' [The foundation stone laying for the Stuttgart building], lecture of 13 January 1911 in *Bilder okkulter Siegel und Säulen. Der Münchener Kongress Pfingsten 1907 und seine Auswirkungen* [Images of esoteric seals and columns: The Whitsun Munich congress, 1907, and its consequences] (GA 284), p. 140.
8. Marie Steiner-von Sivers to Edouard Schuré (31 January 1911) in *Nachrichten der Rudolf Steiner Nachlassverwaltung* [News of the Rudolf Steiner Nachlassverwaltung], vol. 9 (Easter, 1963), p. 13.
9. Ibid., letter of 1 June 1911, p. 14.

10. *Bilder okkulter Siegel und Säulen. Der Münchener Kongress Pfingsten 1907 und seine Auswirkungen* [Images of esoteric seals and columns: The Whitsun Munich congress, 1907, and its consequences] (GA 284), p. 151.

11. *Das esoterische Christentum und die geistige Führung der Menschheit* [Esoteric Christianity and the spiritual guidance of humanity] (GA 130).

12. Ibid., lectures of 27 and 28 September 1912 and 18 December 1912.

13. Peter Selg, *Rudolf Steiner und Christian Rosenkreutz* (Arlesheim, 2010). See also Virginia Sease, 'Das esoterische Rosenkreuzertum als kulturbildende Kraft', in *Anthroposophie wird Kunst* [Anthroposophy becomes art], pp. 241f.

14. *Bilder okkulter Siegel und Säulen* (GA 284), p. 158.

15. See Rudolf Steiner, *Esoterische Betrachtungen karmischer Zusammenhänge* [Esoteric observations on karmic connections], vol. 6 (GA 240), lectures of 18, 19 and 20 July 1924.

16. *Bilder okkulter Siegel und Säulen* (GA 284), pp. 158–9.

17. See Rudolf Steiner's notes for Edouard Schuré in Barr (Alsace), September 1907 in *Rudolf Steiner und Marie Steiner-von Sivers, Briefwechsel und Dokumente 1901–1925* [Rudolf Steiner/Marie Steiner-von Sivers: correspondence and documents 1901–1925] (GA 262).

18. See *Mitteilungen für die Mitglieder der Deutschen Sektion der Theosophischen Gesellschaft (1905–1913) und für die Mitglieder der Anthroposophischen Gesellschaft (1913–1914)* [Newsletter for members of the German Section of the Theosophical Society (1905–1913) and for members of the Anthroposophical Society (1913–1914), ed. Mathilde Scholl, III (August 1906).

19. Ibid.

20. Rudolf Steiner, 'An die sämtlichen Mitglieder der deutschen Sektion der Theosophischen Gesellschaft' [To all members of the German Section of the Theosophical Society], 12 March 1907 in *Zur Geschichte und aus den Inhalten der ersten Abteilung der Esoterischen Schule von 1904 bis 1914* [On the history of the first section of the Esoteric School 1904–1914, and from its contents] (GA 264), p. 294.

21. Ibid.

22. See ibid., p. 480, for a short biography of Annie Besant.

23. Ekkehart Meffert, *Mathilde Scholl und die Geburt der Anthroposophischen Gesellschaft* [Mathilde Scholl and the birth of the Anthroposophical Society] (Dornach 1991), p. 96.

24. See Rudolf Steiner, *Aus den Inhalten der esoterischen Stunden* [From the contents of the esoteric lessons] (GA 266/3), esoteric lesson of 20 October 1905, p. 340.

25. *Anthroposophie wird Kunst.*

26. Rudolf Steiner, *Aus den Inhalten der esoterischen Stunden* [From the contents of the esoteric lessons] (GA 266/1), esoteric lesson of 1 June 1907, p. 221, and esoteric lesson of 4 July 1909, p. 497.

27. See *Aus dem Leben von Marie Steiner-von Sivers* [From the life of Marie Steiner-von Sivers], ed. Hella Wiesberger (Dornach 1956), p. 49.

28. *Zur Geschichte und aus den Inhalten der ersten Abteilung der Esoterischen Schule von 1904 bis 1914* [On the history of the first section of the Esoteric School 1904–1914, and from its contents] (GA 264), Annie Besant to Dr Wilhelm Hübbe-Schleiden, p. 270.

29. See *Mitteilungen für die Mitglieder der Deutschen Sektion der Theosophischen Gesellschaft (1905–1913) und für die Mitglieder der Anthroposophischen Gesellschaft (1913–1914)* [Newsletter for members of the German Section of the Theosophical Society (1905–1913) and for members of the Anthroposophical Society (1913–1914)], ed. Mathilde Scholl, X, January 1910, p. 129.

30. See *Veritas*, 'Mrs. Besant and the Alcyone Case' (Madras, 1913). The reason for the publication is found in the foreword: 'This book is published with a view to assist Mr. Narayaniah to pay the heavy costs of the trial instituted by him in the High Court of Madras for the recovery of his two minor sons— G. Krishnamurthi and G. Nityananda—from Mrs. Annie Besant ... the book contains a full, although necessarily condensed, account of the now famous trial of "G. Narayaniah vs. Annie Besant".'

31. Evelyne Blau, *Krishnamurti 100 Years* (New York 1995), p. 17.

32. Ibid. p. 19. This call first appeared in *The Adyar Bulletin*, December 1911. Evelyne Blau evaluates the situation at the time as follows (p. 20): 'Rudolf Steiner, an eminent Theosophical colleague of Mrs. Besant in Germany, felt that the T.S. was becoming "Orientalized" and refused to accept the boy Krishnamurti as having any kind of spiritual importance. He broke away and formed his own society, Anthroposophy, which flourishes to this day with an emphasis on education, the arts, and publication of books.'

33. Lorenzo Ravagli, 'Theosophie und Anthroposophie—Zur Geschichte einer spannungsreichen Beziehung' [Theosophy and anthroposophy—the history of a tense relationship] in *Anthroposophie wird Kunst.*

34. *Krishnamurti 100 Years*, p. 85.

35. *Mitteilungen für die Mitglieder der Deutschen Sektion der Theosophischen Gesellschaft (1905–1913) und für die Mitglieder der Anthroposophischen Gesellschaft (1913–1914)* XII (November 1911), pp. 172–3.

36. Carl Unger, *Wider literarisches Freibeutertum* [Against literary piracy], Berlin 1913.

37. *Das esoterische Christentum*, foreword by Marie Steiner, p. 11.

38. I am indebted to the Neuchâtel branch leader, Marc Desaules, General Secretary of the Anthroposophical Society in Switzerland, who placed at my disposal materials on the history of the branch. The following description provides a picture of the branch's founding. The notes come from the archive of Rodolphe Christen, who became a member of the Anthroposophical Society in January 1924 and a member of the First Class of the School for Spiritual Science in August 1924:

On 25 August 1959 Madame Berthe Hotz, Monsieur Christen's mother-in-law, attempted to recall the founding of the branch: 'Dr Rudolf Steiner gave lectures at the home of Monsieur Petz, a violinist, who lived in the Rue du Bassin 6 (near Baillod) in Neuchâtel. We find notes about the presence of Mademoiselle Aimee Laval, Madame Levy, Böse, the ladies from Bern (as they were known), Hirter, Schieb, Pestalozzi (?), Mme Grosheintz, Mademoiselle Guye and her brother, Madame Bernard ... and a few Germans who had travelled with the Doctor, Countess Kalckreuth, Fräulein Stinde ... The Doctor arrived by car. He came with Fräulein von Sivers, Fräulein Waller (later Frau Pyle), the wife of Maier who painted the stage curtain for the Goetheanum.' ... The meeting took place in the *Feuillee*; about twenty people had been invited. Among the members was Mademoiselle Charlotte Guye, a person of great importance who studied ancient languages in Paris, Sanskrit among them. She enthralled the audience in the *Feuillee* with her stories about the knights of the Round Table and Parzival. She was a friend of Edouard Schuré, and Madame Coroze-Rihouet said of her: 'A person who made an impression on me second only to Rudolf Steiner.' According to a tradition passed down from 1942, she was the one whom Rudolf Steiner asked about whether the branch might not be called the Christian Rosenkreutz Branch.

39. *Aus den Inhalten der esoterischen Stunden* (GA 266/1), esoteric lesson of 1 June 1907, where Master Jesus is also a leader of the Western esoteric school along with Rudolf Steiner.

40. *Die Theosophie des Rosenkreuzers* [The theosophy of the Rosicrucian] (GA 99).

41. Ibid., lecture of 22 May 1907.

42. *Das esoterische Christentum* (GA130), lecture of 27 September 1911, p. 57.

43. Rudolf Steiner, *Die Tempellegende und die Goldene Legende als symbolischer Ausdruck vergangener und zukünftiger Entwicklungsgeheimnisse des Menschen* [The Temple Legend and the Golden Legend as a symbolic expression of past and future Mysteries in the development of mankind] (GA 93).

44. *Anthroposophie wird Kunst*, p. 243.

45. *Das esoterische Christentum* (GA130), p. 230.

46. Ibid., lecture of 27 September 1911, p. 64.

47. See *Briefwechsel und Dokumente 1901–1925* (GA 262); and *Das Prinzip der spirituellen Ökonomie im Zusammenhang mit Wiederverkörperungsfragen* [The principle of spiritual economy in connection with questions of reincarnation] (GA 109/111), lectures of 28 March 1909 and 11 April 1909.

48. See Virginia Sease, 'Die Ostertagung am Goetheanum und die Weltlage heute. Zur Aktualität der *Chymischen Hochzeit des Christian Rosenkreutz*' [The Easter conference at the Goetheanum and the modern state of the world. On the relevance of *The Chymical Wedding of Christian Rosenkreutz*]

in *Was in der Anthroposophischen Gesellschaft vorgeht, Nachrichten für deren Mitglieder* [What is happening in the Anthroposophical Society, newsletter for its members], Nr. 15, 13 April 2003.

49. *Das esoterische Christentum* (GA130), p. 67.
50. See Virginia Sease, *News for Members of the Anthroposophical Society in America* (2008, No. 1), as well as *Die Tempellegende* (GA 93), p. 307, note 64.
51. *Die Tempellegende* (GA 93), lecture of 4 November 1904, p. 64.
52. See *Das esoterische Christentum* (GA 130), p. 68.
53. *Mitteilungen*, XIII (March 1912), pp. 215–17.
54. For the biography of Baron Carl Alphonse Walleen Bornemann, see Bodo von Plato (ed.), *Anthroposophie im 20. Jahrhundert. Ein Kulturimpuls in biographischen Porträts* [Anthroposophy in the 20th century. A cultural impulse in biographical portraits] (Dornach 2003), and Marie Steiner, 'In memoriam', *Nachrichten für die Mitglieder der Anthroposophischen Gesellschaft* [News for the members of the Anthroposophical Society], 1941:15.
55. *Mitteilungen*, III, pp. 219–20.
56. Rudolf Steiner, *Die befruchtende Wirkung der Anthroposophie auf die Fachwissenschaften* [The fructifying effect of anthroposophy in the professional disciplines] (GA 76), lecture of 8 April 1921, Dornach 1977, p. 196. See also note 195, pp. 255–6.
57. *Anthroposophie im 20. Jahrhundert*, p. 971 and pp. 976–7. A more detailed description of the Johannes Building Association would take us beyond the limits of our topic.
58. *Anthroposophie, Psychosophie, Pneumatosophie* [Anthroposophy, psychosophy, pneumatosophy] (GA 115), foreword by Marie Steiner to the first edition (1931), pp. 304f.
59. *Menschengeschichte im Lichte der Geistesforschung* [Human history in the light of spiritual research] (GA 61).
60. *Faust, der strebende Mensch, Geisteswissenschaftliche Erläuterungen zu Goethes Faust* [Faust, the striving human being, spiritual-scientific annotations to Goethe's *Faust*], vol. I (GA 272), lecture of 17 December 1911, p. 39.
61. *Die Mission der neuen Geistesoffenbarung. Das Christus-Ereignis als Mittelpunktsgeschehen der Erdenevolution* [The mission of the new revelation of the spirit. The Christ event as the central event of Earth evolution] (GA 127), lecture of 19 December 1911.
62. Ibid., lecture of 21 December 1911, p. 222.
63. *Aus den Inhalten der esoterischen Stunden* [From the contents of the esoteric lessons] (GA 266/2), lesson of 16 December 1911.
64. *Zur Geschichte und aus den Inhalten der erkenntniskultischen Abteilung der Esoterischen Schule von 1904 bis 1914* [On the history of the cognitive-cultic section of the Esoteric School 1904–1914, and from its contents] (GA 265), lesson of 16 December 1911, pp. 94–5.
65. *Aus dem Leben von Marie Steiner-von Sivers*, pp. 404f.
66. Ibid. p. 418.

67. See Hella Wiesberger, *Marie Steiner-von Sivers. Ein Leben für die Anthroposophie. Eine biographische Dokumentation* [Marie Steiner-von Sivers. A life for anthroposophy. A biographical documentation] (Dornach, 1988), p. 220.

68. *Zur Geschichte und aus den Inhalten der ersten Abteilung der Esoterischen Schule* (GA 264), p. 423.

69. *Rudolf Steiner und Marie Steiner-von Sivers, Briefwechsel und Dokumente 1901–1925* (GA 262), notes on p. 480 and p. 483.

70. *Zur Geschichte und aus den Inhalten der ersten Abteilung der Esoterischen Schule* (GA 264), p. 423.

71. I was able to have several conversations in the 1990s with Ruth Barnett Pusch. A helpful resource is Hans Pusch, *A New Kind of Actor: Letters about Marie Steiner and her Work with Actors on the Stage of the Goetheanum in the 1930s*, translated and edited by Ruth Pusch (New York 1998).

72. *Zur Geschichte und aus den Inhalten der ersten Abteilung der Esoterischen Schule* (GA 264), p. 425.

73. Ibid. p. 426.

74. Ibid.

75. Ibid. p. 425.

76. Ibid. p. 426.

77. Ibid.

78. Ibid. p. 427.

79. Ibid. pp. 427–8.

80. Rudolf Steiner, *Die Tempellegende und die Goldene Legende als symbolischer Ausdruck vergangener und zukünftiger Entwicklungsgeheimnisse des Menschen*, GA 93, p. 64.

81. Rudolf Steiner, *Das christliche Mysterium* [The Christian mystery] (GA 97), lecture of 16 February 1907, p. 216.

82. *Die Erkenntnis des Übersinnlichen in unserer Zeit und deren Bedeutung für das heutige Leben* [Knowledge of the supersensible in our time and its meaning for modern life] (GA 55), lecture of 14 March 1907, p. 176.

83. *Die Menschheitsentwickelung und Christus-Erkenntnis* [The development of humanity and knowledge of the Christ] (GA 100), lecture of 16 June 1907, p. 21.

84. *Zur Geschichte und aus den Inhalten der ersten Abteilung der Esoterischen Schule* (GA 264), pp. 426–7.

85. Ibid. p. 427.

86. Ibid.

87. Ibid. p. 428.

88. Ibid.

89. Ibid. p. 429.

90. Ibid.

91. Ibid. pp. 417–18.

92. Ibid. pp. 429–30.

93. *Zur Geschichte und aus den Inhalten der erkenntniskultischen Abteilung der Esoterischen Schule von 1904 bis 1914* (GA 265), Ritualtext für die Logeneröffnung [Ritual text for the opening of the lodge], p. 153.

94. *Zur Geschichte und aus den Inhalten der ersten Abteilung der Esoterischen Schule* (GA 264), p. 430.

95. Ibid. pp. 430–1.

96. *Probleme des Zusammenlebens in der Anthroposophischen Gesellschaft, Dokumente zur Dornacher Krise vom Jahre 1915* [Problems of community life in the Anthroposophical Society, documents related to the 1915 crisis in Dornach] (GA 253), pp. 125–6.

97. *Briefwechsel und Dokumente 1901–1925* (GA 262), pp. 180–1.

98. Wilfried Hammacher, *Die Uraufführung der Mysteriendramen von und durch Rudolf Steiner München 1910–1913* [The premiere of the Mystery Dramas by and through Rudolf Steiner Munich 1910–1913 (Dornach, 2010), p. 281.

99. Ellic Howe, *The Magicians of the Golden Dawn. A Documentary. History of a Magical Order 1887–1923* (York Beach, Maine, 1984), p. 281.

100. Ibid. p. 282.

101. Ibid.

102. Ibid.

103. Ibid.

104. Kenneth Mackenzie, *The Royal Masonic Cyclopaedia* (Wellingborough, Northamptonshire, 1987).

105. See *Bilder okkulter Siegel und Säulen* (GA 284).

106. See Manfred Lurker, *Wörterbuch der Symbolik* (Stuttgart 1988).

107. *Der Orient im Lichte des Okzidents: Die Kinder des Luzifer und die Brüder Christi* [The Orient in the light of the Occident: The children of Lucifer and the brothers of Christ] (GA 113), lecture of 31 August 1909, p. 191.

108. Ibid. p. 192.

109. *Zur Geschichte und aus den Inhalten der ersten Abteilung der Esoterischen Schule* (GA 264), p. 427.

110. *Die okkulte Bewegung im 19. Jahrhundert und ihre Beziehung zur Weltkultur* [The occult movement in the 19th century and its relation to world culture] (GA 254), lecture of 18 October 1915, p. 98.

111. *Vier Mysteriendramen* [Four Mystery Dramas] (GA 14), pp. 489f.

112. Ibid.

113. *The Soul's Awakening*, Scene 8, p. 106, in Rudolf Steiner, *Four Mystery Plays*, trans. Ruth and Hans Pusch (SteinerBooks/Anthroposophic Press, 2007).

114. Ibid.

115. Ibid.

116. *Zur Geschichte und aus den Inhalten der ersten Abteilung der Esoterischen Schule* (GA 264), p. 431.

117. Ibid. pp. 430–1.

118. Ibid.

119. Ibid.

120. Ibid. p. 431.

121. In early 2012 the cited documents from Uwe Werner will appear in a book edited by Robin Schmidt.

122. *Zur Geschichte und aus den Inhalten der ersten Abteilung der Esoterischen Schule* (GA 264), p. 421.

123. Florian Roder, 'Persönlichkeiten im Umkreis des Münchener Kongresses' [Personalties connected with the Munich congress] in *Was in der Anthroposophischen Gesellschaft vorgeht*, Nr. 49, 7 December 2007.

124. *Unsere Toten. Ansprachen, Gedenkworte und Meditationssprüche 1906–1924* [Our dead. Addresses, eulogies, and meditative verses] (GA 261), Address at the cremation of Sophie Stinde, pp. 157 and 159.

125. Roder in *Was in der Anthroposophischen Gesellschaft vorgeht*, Nr. 50, 14 December 2007.

126. Marie Steiner, 'In memoriam Imme von Eckardtstein', in *Was in der Anthroposophischen Gesellschaft vorgeht*, Nr. 20, 1930, p. 78.

127. Ibid. p. 79. See also *Anthroposophie im 20. Jahrhundert*, biographical entry for Imme von Eckardtstein by Linda Blumenthal.

128. *Anthroposophie im 20. Jahrhundert*, biographical entry for Hermann Linde by Elisabeth Bessau.

129. *Unsere Toten* (GA 261), Address at the cremation of Hermann Linde, p. 264.

130. Ibid. pp. 272 and 274.

131. *Anthroposophie im 20. Jahrhundert*, biographical entry for Adolf Arenson by Ronald Templeton.

132. See Christian Ginat on Adolf Arenson in *Verzeichnis musikalischer Werke* (Dornach 1987).

133. Carl Unger, *Schriften* [Works], vol. 1 (Stuttgart 1964), pp. 322f.

134. See *Anthroposophie im 20. Jahrhundert*, biographical entry for Carl Unger by Renatus Ziegler; the entry provides a comprehensive bibliography of Unger's works and secondary literature.

135. *Philosophie und Anthroposophie, Gesammelte Aufsätze 1904–1923* [Philosophy and anthroposophy, collected essays, 1904–1923] (GA 35), pp. 93–4.

136. *Zur Geschichte und aus den Inhalten der ersten Abteilung der Esoterischen Schule* (GA 264), index of persons with biographical notes, pp. 447f. See also *Anthroposophie im 20. Jahrhundert*.

137. *Zur Geschichte und aus den Inhalten der ersten Abteilung der Esoterischen Schule* (GA 264), p. 471.

138. *Zur Geschichte und aus den Inhalten der erkenntniskultischen Abteilung der Esoterischen Schule von 1904 bis 1914* [On the history of the cognitive-cultic section of the Esoteric School 1904–1914, and from its contents] (GA 265); The Rosicrucian ending, p. 163 (p. 166 in the older version of GA 265).

139. Ibid. p. 427.

140. *Die Tempellegende* (GA 93), lecture of 22 October 1905, p. 209.

141. *Zur Geschichte und aus den Inhalten der ersten Abteilung der Esoterischen Schule* (GA 264), p. 426.

142. Ibid. p. 430.

143. Ibid. p. 427.

144. Ibid. pp. 427–8.

145. Ibid. p. 429.

146. *Was in der Anthroposophischen Gesellschaft vorgeht*, 5 October 1924.

147. *Zur Geschichte und aus den Inhalten der ersten Abteilung der Esoterischen Schule* (GA 264), p. 428.

148. Ibid. p. 429.

149. *Die Theosophie des Rosenkreuzers* (GA 99), lecture of 22 May 1907, p. 15.

150. *Wie erlangt man Erkenntnisse der höheren Welten?* [How to attain knowledge of higher worlds] (GA 10).

151. See *Oxford Universal English Dictionary*, ed. William Little, H.W. Fowler, J. Coulson, revised edition (Oxford, 1955).

152. *Zur Geschichte und aus den Inhalten der ersten Abteilung der Esoterischen Schule* (GA 264), p. 429.

153. Ibid.

154. Ibid.

155. Ibid.

156. Ibid. p. 431.

157. Ibid. p. 433.

158. Ibid.

159. Ibid.

160. Ibid. p. 435.

161. *The Soul's Probation*, Scene 9, p. 105 in *Four Mystery Dramas*.

162. *Zur Geschichte und aus den Inhalten der ersten Abteilung der Esoterischen Schule* (GA 264), p. 434.

163. Ibid.

164. Ibid. p. 435.

165. *Probleme des Zusammenlebens in der Anthroposophischen Gesellschaft* (GA 253), lecture of 21 August 1915, p. 150.

166. Ibid.

167. Ibid. p. 126. Here it is mentioned that Alice Sprengel claims to have been the 'inspirer' of Rudolf Steiner's 'spiritual teaching'.

168. Ibid. pp. 132–3.

169. Ibid. p. 149.

170. Ibid. pp.149–50.

171. Ibid. p. 79.

172. Ibid. p. 190.

173. *Die spirituellen Hintergrunde der aüßeren Welt. Der Sturz der Geister der Finsternis.* [The spiritual background of the exoteric world. The fall of the spirits of darkness] (GA 177), lecture of 30 September 1917, p. 37.

174. *Philosophie und Anthroposophie* (GA 35), pp. 471–2, note 336.

175. *Zur Geschichte und aus den Inhalten der ersten Abteilung der Esoterischen Schule* (GA 264), pp. 421–2.

176. Ibid. p. 429.

177. A book to be published by the Forschungsstelle Kulturimpuls, Goetheanum, in early 2012 (ed. Robin Schmidt), will also deal with the theme of the 1911 Endowment. Uwe Werner is collaborating as well.

178. Rudolf Steiner, cited from the 1912/1913 *Calendar* (Berlin 1912). The first part of the Calendar has a drawing by Imme von Eckardtstein with the dates for important people supplied by Rudolf Steiner for each day of the month. See also *Der Anthroposophische Seelenkalender und der Kalender 1912/1913 in Beiträge zur Rudolf Steiner Gesamtausgabe*, No. 37/38, Spring/Summer 1972.

179. *Wahrspruchworte* [Verses and meditations] (GA 40) 'Foreword to the Second Edition 1918', p. 20.

180. *Zur Geschichte und aus den Inhalten der ersten Abteilung der Esoterischen Schule* (GA 264), p. 428.

181. There is no complete record of this address, only notes by various people who had attended. Only the stenographic notes made by Berta Reebstein-Lehmann were available and used for the version published by Marie Steiner in 1947 which she based on her own notes and recollections. Notes by Mieta Pyler-Waller and Elisabeth Vreede found later formed the basis for supplements and amendments incorporated into the 1984 edition. The notes by Mieta Pyler-Waller were reviewed by Rudolf Steiner himself and adjusted with a few corrections. Based on Franz Seiler's more extensive stenographic notes which were initially transcribed for the first edition of GA 264, *Zur Geschichte und aus den Inhalten der ersten Abteilung der Esoterischen Schule 1904–1914* [About the history and from the content of the first department of the esoteric school 1904–1914], it was possible to supplement these documents further.

182. This is Marie Steiner's foreword to the 1947 edition of Rudolf Steiner's address. It was privately published and distributed by her in mimeographed form.

183. Translators' note: To understand this statement in context, it must be recalled that Marie Steiner wrote this introduction two years after the end of the Second World War, an era when Europe and much of the anthroposophical movement still lay in ruins.

184. It was pointed out at the opening of the Christmas Conference in the lecture on 24 December 1923 that the impulse for the anthroposophical movement had flowed 'not out of earthly will but in accord with the call that had sounded out of the spiritual world'.

185. This more intimate circle existed within the Esoteric School.

186. The lecture of 22 October 1905 (GA 93) is presumably meant here; it was held in Berlin for the Annual General Meeting [of the Theosophical Society—*Translators*] at that time.